THE STORY OF
MUSIC

VOLUME 1

Classical Music
from Earliest Times

GROLIER
EDUCATIONAL

ABOUT THIS BOOK

This book is one of a set of ten that tells the story of music from earliest times to the present day. Starting with the primitive sounds made by the crude instruments devised by early human beings, the first book traces the development of music through the centuries, describing how it evolved and how musical instruments became more refined and ever more capable of delivering beautiful sounds. The second book in the series focuses on the music of the 19th and 20th centuries, showing how the orchestra developed to become the impressively large body that it is today, and how composers ranged through a variety of musical styles, culminating in the exciting electronic experiments of the late 20th century.

Other volumes in the series look at music from around the world and U.S. music in the forms of folk, country, and Cajun, as well as gospel, blues, and jazz. A whole volume examines modern music, from rock 'n' roll to hip-hop. Another book looks at musicals, operetta, and film music, while music education and the music business are also given an entire volume. A whole book focuses on musical instruments and recording technology, while the final book in the series looks at the voice, opera, songs, and singing in general.

The books are fully illustrated, and each volume ends with a timeline, a glossary of musical terms and notation, a list of further reading, and a comprehensive index covering the complete set.

Published 2001 by Grolier Educational
Sherman Turnpike
Danbury, Connecticut 06816

© 2001 Brown Partworks Ltd

Set ISBN: 0-7172-9559-1
Volume ISBN: 0-7172-9560-5

Library of Congress Cataloging-in-Publication Data
Story of music
    p. cm.
    Includes indexes.
    Contents: v. 1. Classical music from earliest times -- v. 2. Classical music: romantic to modern -- v. 3. Music from around the world -- v. 4. Folk, country, and cajun music -- v. 5. Gospel, blues, and jazz - - v. 6. From rock and pop to hip-hop -- v. 7. Music of stage and screen -- v. 8. The music profession -- v. 9. Musical instruments and technology -- v. 10. The voice and song.
    ISBN 0-7172-9559-1 (set: alk. paper) -- ISBN 0-7172-9560-5 (v. 1: alk. paper) -- ISBN 0-7179-9561-3 (v. 2: alk. paper) -- ISBN 0-7172-9562-1 (v. 3: alk. paper) -- ISBN 0-7172-9563-X (v. 4: alk. paper) -- ISBN 0-7172-9564-8 (v. 5: alk. paper) -- ISBN 0-7172-9565-6 (v. 6: alk. paper) -- ISBN 0-7172-9566-4 (v. 7: alk. paper) -- ISBN 0-7172-9567-2 (v. 8: alk. paper) -- ISBN 0-7172-9568-0 (v. 9: alk. paper) -- ISBN 0-7172-9569-9 (v. 10: alk. paper)
    1. Music--History and criticism--Juvenile literature. [Music-- History and criticism.]
ML3928 .S76 2000
780--dc21

00-023220

For information address the publisher:
Grolier Educational, Sherman Turnpike,
Danbury, Connecticut 06816

Printed in Singapore

Glossary
Words that are explained in the glossary are printed in **bold** type the first time they appear in a chapter.

FOR BROWN PARTWORKS LTD

Editor: Julian Flanders
Deputy editor: Sally McFall
Design: Kelly-Anne Levey
Picture research: Helen Simm

Managing editor: Lindsey Lowe
Production: Matt Weyland

Contributor: Barrie Carson Turner
Consultant: Michael Weber

PHOTOGRAPHIC CREDITS
Front cover: Medieval musicians, **Mary Evans Picture Library**.
Title page: Dancing at the court of Queen Elizabeth I, **The Lebrecht Collection**. **AKG London**: 25tl, 26b, 35, 40, 42, 44br, 46bc, 47, 53, 56t, 67bl; **The Ancient Egypt Picture Library**: 6tl; **The Art Archive**: 11, 20, 41b, 43b, 54b; **The Bridgeman Art Library**: 52; **Corbis**: Archivo Iconografico 17, 28, 55, 56b, 62, Arte & Immagini srl 8br, Austrian Archives 59, David Bartoff 49, Gianni Dagli Orti 19tr, David Lees 15, 31t, Araldo de Luca 14, National Gallery 27b, 57tr, Keren Su 6, Francesco Venturi 32c, Kea Publishing Services Ltd 32; **Mary Evans Picture Library**: 8tr, 13, 16, 18, 19cl, 24, 46tc, 54t, 57bl, 60, 63t, Explorer Archive 41t, 44tl, Edwin Wallace 7; **Hulton Getty**: 9, 10, 12, 25bc, 29t, 34bl, 36t, 37t&b, 39, 43t, 45, 48, 51tr, 63br, 64, 67tl; **The Lebrecht Collection**: 22, 23tl&br, 26t, 27t, 29b, 30, 31b, 33, 34br, 36b, 38, 51bl, 58, 61bl; **Werner Forman Archive**: 50, Museum für Völkerkunde Berlin 5b, Tanzania National Museum 4b.
Pages 4&5t courtesy of Dr. Ivan Turk, Institute of Archaeology, Slovenian Academy of Sciences.
Key: b=below, t=top, c=center, l=left, r=right.
Every effort has been made to trace copyright holders and gain permission for material reproduced in this volume. We regret if any errors have occurred.

Maps and artworks: Colin Woodman
Musical notation: Harry Boteler

Contents

VOLUME 1

Classical Music from Earliest Times

A World of Sound   4

A Rebirth   20

A Misshapen Pearl   32

The Classical Era   50

Timeline   *68*

Glossary   *70*

Musical Notation and Further Reading   *72*

Index   *73*

CHAPTER 1

A World of Sound

An awareness of the sounds of nature—whether the cry of an animal or the whistle of the wind—and the desire to imitate and interpret them is the beginning of the story of music.

The world has always been filled with sound. Primitive peoples were surrounded by the many sounds of nature: the scream of an animal in pain, the roar of a waterfall, the gurgle of a brook, or the whistle of the wind. Their awareness of these sounds, and the desire to imitate and interpret them, is the beginning of the story of music.

Many of these early sounds caused fear in the listener. The growl of an unknown animal in the night or a violent crack of thunder was frightening. Animals—even large, dangerous ones—could also be frightened by sound. People soon found that by banging sticks and stones together, animals could be scared away. Human enemies too could be frightened by noise, especially if yelping and whooping voices were added to the clattering of sticks and stones. Such a show of noise was also a show of strength and determination.

When the enemy fled, these sounds would rise to shouts of joyous celebration. This noise of celebration was one of the first types of music ever made. Similar sounds were made at other celebrations, such as during the killing of an animal that would provide food for several days. Members of the tribe who were not equipped with noisemaking sticks or stones could slap their bodies or stamp their feet. Moving around or rocking to and fro—dancing— became a natural accompaniment to these sounds.

The first musical instruments

The first musical instruments were shaped by nature. Sticks and smooth stones could be struck together, and logs or even the trunks of trees could be beaten with sticks to create sound.

Above: This fragment of bone is probably part of an ancient flute. It was found in Slovenia in Eastern Europe and is thought to be about 43,000 years old.

Below: A Stone Age painting from Tanzania, Africa, shows dancers at a celebration.

People also found that the sounds were different depending on what objects they used. Bones produced a crisp "chuck" when banged together. Large logs made a dull, heavy thud, which traveled a long distance and could be used to communicate over larger areas.

People living near the sea discovered that shells too could make a noise. A damaged shell such as a conch, with the spiral end missing, would make a sound when air was blown through it. Bones and stones often had natural cracks and holes in them that could also produce a sound when blown through. These natural objects became the first crude flutes, whistles, and trumpets.

Man-made instruments

But why wait for nature to fashion the shape and sound-making qualities of these objects? It was not that difficult to punch holes through shells and soft bones. Wood too could be easily shaped with simple tools. And it was also very easy to knock the end off a large conch shell to make a blowhole. This is how the first musical instruments were made.

As human civilization developed, so did people's ability to create more complex instruments. By the time of the great ancient civilizations of Egypt, China, Greece, and Rome, each society had developed its own types of musical instruments and its own forms of music. But the one thing that these peoples had in common was how important music had become in all of their lives.

Music in ancient Egypt

In Egypt at the time of the ancient kings known as pharaohs, music occupied a leading position in everyday life. It was particularly important in religious rituals, but was also used for entertainment. Egyptian **lyrics** (the words of songs) were usually about love, shepherds tending their flocks, or men working in the fields. Such lyrics, along with musicians playing instruments, have been found engraved on the sides of ancient Egyptian tombs. Sometimes the names of the instruments were written above the paintings.

The ancient Greeks and Romans both admitted to being influenced by the Egyptians—especially in music. From as early as 3000 B.C. the Egyptians had end-blown flutes (like the modern recorder). They also played pipes similar to the clarinet, as well as oboes, harps, and trumpets. Percussion instruments included the *sistrum* (a type of rattle), drums, tambourines, and clappers (like modern-day castanets).

Right: A drinking vessel from about 205–650 A.D. shows a man blowing a conch shell.

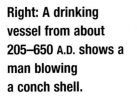

Many ancient Egyptian instruments have survived to the present day. Most famous of all are the two magnificent trumpets—one bronze and one silver—that were found by the explorer Howard Carter in 1922 in the tomb of Tutankhamun (*c.*1340–1323 B.C.).

Music in ancient China

In ancient China, as in Egypt, music was a basic element in daily life and in every person's education. It formed a major part of religious rituals, court ceremonies, and festivals. Ancient documents still survive that tell us about this fascinating world of music and performance in Chinese life. The philosopher Confucius (551–478 B.C.) stressed the importance of music in education. He believed that music sustained the soul in the way that food sustained the body. Evidence of

Above: The most famous ancient Egyptian musical instruments are these two trumpets found in the tomb of Tutankhamun in the Valley of the Kings.

Above: A group of men playing bamboo *shengs* at a local festival in 1996 in Kaili, China.

The Development of Music

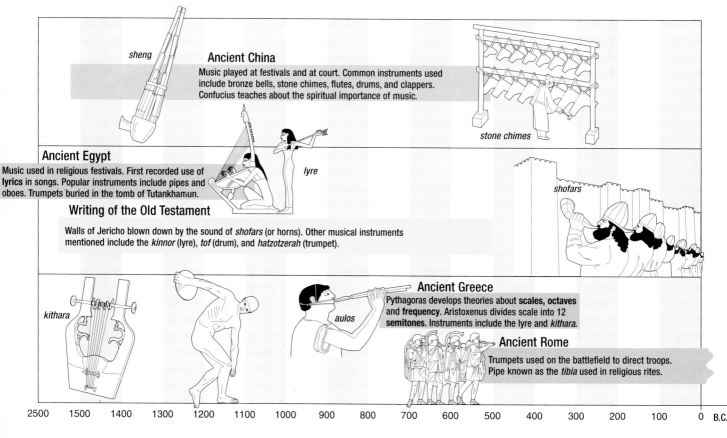

sheng

Ancient China
Music played at festivals and at court. Common instruments used include bronze bells, stone chimes, flutes, drums, and clappers. Confucius teaches about the spiritual importance of music.

stone chimes

Ancient Egypt
Music used in religious festivals. First recorded use of **lyrics** in songs. Popular instruments include pipes and oboes. Trumpets buried in the tomb of Tutankhamun.

lyre

shofars

Writing of the Old Testament
Walls of Jericho blown down by the sound of *shofars* (or horns). Other musical instruments mentioned include the *kinnor* (lyre), *tof* (drum), and *hatzotzerah* (trumpet).

kithara

aulos

Ancient Greece
Pythagoras develops theories about **scales**, **octaves** and **frequency**. Aristoxenus divides scale into 12 **semitones**. Instruments include the lyre and *kithara*.

Ancient Rome
Trumpets used on the battlefield to direct troops. Pipe known as the *tibia* used in religious rites.

| 2500 | 1500 | 1400 | 1300 | 1200 | 1100 | 1000 | 900 | 800 | 700 | 600 | 500 | 400 | 300 | 200 | 100 | 0 B.C. |

A GIFT FROM THE GODS

Many ancient civilizations believed that music was a gift from the gods. In ancient Egypt it was Osiris, the god of the dead, who gave the gift of music to humans. Other Egyptian gods associated with music were Isis (the sister and wife of Osiris), Amun (the god of fertility), and Hathor (the goddess of joy and love, and of the sky).

In India music was the gift of Brahma, the creator of the universe. In China an ancient legend tells of an emperor who wished to know the mystery of music. He sent his minister far to the west of the country to seek out the phoenix bird. When the minister expressed the emperor's wish to the bird, the phoenix told him the secret of music.

According to ancient Greek legend, the first musical instrument was given to humans by Pan, the god of shepherds and sheep. The story tells of his pursuit of a beautiful nymph, Syrinx. When the Ladon River blocked her path and she was trapped, a protecting god transformed her into a reed. From this reed Pan made the first musical instrument—the panpipe.

In ancient Greece Apollo was the god of music. He played the lyre (see page 9), which was associated with wisdom and balance. In a legend from ancient Greece the lyre was invented by Apollo's half-brother Hermes, who gave it to him as a gift to apologize for having stolen some of Apollo's cattle.

Apollo was also the leader of the Muses—the goddesses of astronomy, history, heroic poetry, love poetry, instrumental music, tragedy, comedy, mime, and dancing and choral song—from which the word "music" derives. The muses inspired people to write poetry and songs. The

Above: The god Pan plays the panpipe, which he made from a reed. According to Greek legend, the panpipe was the very first musical instrument.

ancient Greeks used various combinations of these arts and sciences (which they called "the muses") within their musical performances, so the word "music" had a wider interpretation in ancient Greece than it does today.

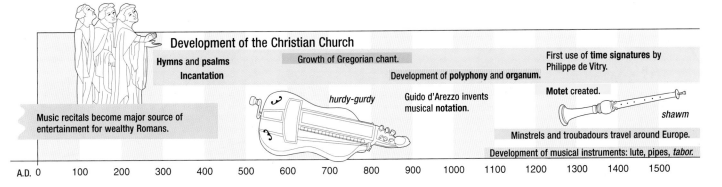

Development of the Christian Church

Hymns and psalms
Incantation

Growth of Gregorian chant.

Development of polyphony and organum.

First use of time signatures by Philippe de Vitry.

Motet created.

hurdy-gurdy

Guido d'Arezzo invents musical notation.

shawm

Music recitals become major source of entertainment for wealthy Romans.

Minstrels and troubadours travel around Europe.

Development of musical instruments: lute, pipes, *tabor.*

A.D. 0   100   200   300   400   500   600   700   800   900   1000   1100   1200   1300   1400   1500

how important music was in ancient China is seen in the many musical instruments that have been found in glittering treasure troves buried in royal tombs from this time.

Some of the most ancient Chinese instruments were bronze bells, stone chimes, oval-shaped flutes (called ocarinas), and drums—all of which were invented by 1400 B.C. Later, new percussion and wind instruments—such as clappers, scrapers, and flutes—emerged. The Chinese mouth organ, the *sheng*, first appeared in about 1100 B.C., although it is said to have been invented 2,000 years earlier by Emperor Nyu-kwa in the image of the phoenix (the vertical pipes suggesting the bird's wings). Ancient Chinese paintings still survive that show noblewomen performing at court on an instrument called the *pipa*, which was similar to the lute. The oldest Chinese stringed instrument, first mentioned in a poem of 1100 B.C., is the long zither—a kind of flat harp.

Music in ancient Greece

Music was fundamental to life in ancient Greece. It was played at religious ceremonies, marriages, funerals, and sports and political events. The philosophers Plato (429–347 B.C.) and Aristotle (384–322 B.C.) believed strongly in a musical education and emphasized this in their writings. Singing and playing in ancient Greek music was entirely monophonic—that is, every performer and instrument played or sang exactly the same **melody**. A melody, or tune, is a series of sounds with

Left: The most popular wind instrument in ancient Greece was the *aulos*, which was similar to the modern oboe. One performer often played two of them at the same time.

ORPHEUS AND HIS LYRE

For the ancient Greeks the legendary figure of Orpheus represented power through music. He was a gifted singer and lyre player, and the son of a Thracian king and one of the Muses. Apollo gave him a lyre and with it the ability to charm all nature with his singing and playing.

The legend goes that the wife of Orpheus, Eurydice, died from a snakebite and went to Hades, the kingdom of the dead. Pluto, King of the Underworld and ruler of Hades, gave Orpheus one last chance, through his playing, to retrieve his wife from the Underworld on the condition that he did not look back at her until they returned to the world above. However, Orpheus was unable to resist a glance back, and so he lost his wife for good. This tragic tale has inspired works by many composers, from Jacopo Peri and Giulio Caccini's opera *Euridice* in 1600 to Igor Stravinsky's ballet *Orpheus* in 1947.

Right: A 16th-century Italian sculpture showing Orpheus playing his lyre.

a distinct musical shape. Skilled performers, however, added their own embellishments, or decorations, to the melody (see page 33).

Ancient Greece had a wealth of different instruments. Many of them were played to accompany the reciting of poetry. The lyre and the *kithara* were the most popular stringed instruments used for this purpose. The lyre was a simpler version of the *kithara* and was usually played for fun at home. It was held upright, or at a slightly slanted angle, and plucked with the fingers or with a **pick** (a small, thin object made of a strong but flexible material that is held between the fingers to pull the strings). The *kithara* was larger and heavier than the lyre, and had a powerful **tone**. It was the instrument played by the working musician.

Ancient Greece had a wealth of different instruments

The most popular wind instrument was the *aulos*, which was similar to the modern oboe. One performer usually played two of them together. The panpipe—a set of flutes made from reeds of different lengths joined together—was used in **folk music** rather than political or festive music.

Brass instruments were generally used in war to pass signals to the troops, since their sound was loud enough to be heard over the noise of the battlefield. The *salpinx* was a straight trumpet, and the *keras* was a member of the horn family.

The ancient Greeks also played a number of percussion instruments, including tambourines, clappers, cymbals, and rattles.

Above: An engraving of various *kitharas* and lyres from ancient Greece with Erato, the Greek muse of love poetry (right), and Apollo, the god of music (left), plucking some of the instruments with a pick. The more elaborate instruments are the *kitharas*.

The Olympic Games

Games and festivals were important to ancient Greeks as arenas where human achievements and excellence of the body and mind were presented before the gods. Music was one of the activities in which it was important to excel. The Olympic Games—a five-day festival held in honor of Zeus, ruler of the Greek gods—included contests in music, dancing, and drama, as well as athletics.

The first Olympic Games were held in 776 B.C. This is also the first fixed date in Greek history, indicating how important these games were to Greek society. The Olympics were eventually held every four years until they were suspended in the fourth century. They were not held again until 1896.

Second to the Olympic Games in importance were the Pythian Games. This grand festival in honor of Apollo included contests for the best lyre player and the writer of the best tune, alongside athletic competitions. The games were held in the Greek city of Delphi. *Paeans* (choral hymns) were sung in praise of Apollo to the accompaniment of the *kithara*, and there was also dancing. Other similar competitions were held in Corinth and Argolis.

this music was that, having heard the sound since birth, they had become completely accustomed to it.

Pythagoras believed that the world was governed by numbers, which he applied to many aspects of music. In his studies of acoustics (the nature of sound) he discovered the numerical vibrations of the main notes of the musical **scale** (a series of single notes moving upward or downward). He focused particularly on the **octave**—the eighth note up or down from any

---

Pythagoras introduced many of the ideas that became the basis of Western music

---

other note. For example, when moving from one octave to the next octave higher, he found that the **frequency**—the measure of a note's pitch according to the number of vibrations it gives off—doubles.

Pythagoras also invented the series of scales called **modes**. These modes were made up of seven scales (C–C, D–D, E–E, F–F, G–G, A–A, and B–B), which, on the keyboard, used only the white notes. The modes were later adopted by composers during the medieval period.

The beginnings of rhythm

The Greek theorist Aristoxenus (*c*.375–320 B.C.), a pupil of the philosopher Aristotle, took the ideas of Pythagoras and other music theorists of the time and organized and simplified them into a system that the common musician could use. He wrote several books on the structure of scales and an important book on **rhythm**, which he was the first to identify as an organization of notes with respect to time.

The father of Western music

Pythagoras (*c*.580–500 B.C.) was a Greek philosopher, mathematician, and religious teacher who introduced many of the ideas that became the basis of Western music. He lived in Greece until about 531 B.C., when he emigrated to southern Italy and founded a religious settlement, a school, and a philosophical society.

Pythagoras believed that mysticism, math, music, and astronomy were all related. One of his more bizarre theories has become known as "the music of the spheres." Pythagoras believed that each planet revolving in its cycle, or "sphere," created its own **note** (a single sound of a given **pitch**) according to the speed of its movement through space. So a celestial music was created from the notes of all the planets sounding together. Pythagoras argued that the reason people were unable to hear

Above: Pythagoras, the Greek philosopher and mathematician who is also known as the father of Western music.

Unlike Pythagoras—who believed that notes could only be measured in mathematical ratios—Aristoxenus was convinced that notes were a continuous, flowing line of high and low sounds that could only be determined by the listener, and that this line could be divided into any convenient number of steps to form a scale. He divided the octave into 12 **semitones**, or half-steps (on the keyboard they are the distances between one note and the next, whether it is black or white). This structure remains the basis of Western music today.

Music in ancient Rome

The ancient Romans were greatly influenced by the role of music in other cultures, especially that of ancient Greece, and inherited many instruments and practices from other civilizations. Music played a major part in war, funerals, religious ceremonies, political and sports events, entertainment, and even work.

On the battlefield trumpets were used to signal attacks and retreats, and horns were added to the trumpets to overwhelm or confuse the enemy. Solo singing, accompanied by an instrument such as the *kithara* or lyre, was an important form of entertainment for the privileged classes and was performed by anyone from slaves to the Roman emperors themselves (the emperors Nero and Caligula were both known to perform for their guests). Singing and instrumental music were also used by workers as rhythmic accompaniment to such repetitive activities as rowing, reaping, weaving, or treading grapes to make wine. It was even thought that music played to Roman athletes while they were training helped increase their strength and endurance.

Below: A musician is shown entertaining guests with his music at a banquet in this Roman mosaic.

Music also held unique magical possibilities to the Romans. The Roman wind instrument the *tibia*, in particular, was linked with these magical powers. It was originally a pipe made from an inner leg bone located between the knee and the ankle (still called the tibia) with three or four finger holes punched into it. Later it became a double-piped instrument made of wood, ivory, or silver. The *tibia* was used in both the theater and in religious rites. During religious ceremonies its powerful sound drowned out the grim noises of animals being slaughtered in sacrifice. It was also used to banish evil spirits and summon good ones. Because of

The ancient Romans were greatly influenced by the music of other cultures

the important role of the *tibia* in Roman society, its players were held in high esteem. They were allowed to have special privileges and held a procession and great feast in Rome once a year.

Music in the Old Testament

Music is mentioned often in the Bible, but detailed descriptions of instruments are rarely given. Since the ancient texts are not illustrated, it is almost always difficult to know precisely which instruments are meant from their descriptions. Also, the Old Testament was written over a period stretching from about 2000 B.C. to 500 B.C., which allowed plenty of time for any instrument to go through changes in both name and appearance.

Music scholars, however, after extensive research are reasonably certain about the descriptions of some instruments. The *kinnor*, one of the first instruments mentioned in the Bible (in the book of Genesis), is the modern Hebrew name for the violin. In its biblical context, though, it was almost certainly a lyre—an instrument on which King David excelled. It is also the instrument the Jews refused to play "in a strange land" during their exile in Babylon.

The *tof* is the only drum to be mentioned in the Bible. It is a frame drum, like the tambourine (but without jingles), and was usually played by women. It was used along with singing and dancing, and was probably the "*timbrel*" played by Miriam after the crossing of the Red Sea. Another instrument found in the Bible is the *hatzotzerah*—a type of trumpet. Moses was commanded to make "two trumpets of silver." They were made from one sheet of metal and would have been similar to the trumpets that were found in Tutankhamun's tomb.

The *shofar*, traditionally a ram's horn, is probably the most famous of all the instruments of the Bible and the only biblical instrument that is still played today. It is first mentioned in

Below: A 19th-century painting showing David playing the lyre for King Saul.

THE ROLE OF THE MONASTERIES IN MUSIC

During the days when Christians were persecuted they were often forced to take refuge in remote places. It was in these out-of-the-way places that the first religious colonies, or monasteries, developed.

The first Western monastic order was founded by St. Benedict (*c.*480–547) and its members were called Benedictines. It spread across Europe and gave rise to other holy orders. The monks worked together to provide their own food and became leaders in agriculture and technology. As they found better ways to farm the land, they began to have more time on their hands. So when the pressure of agricultural work was not too great, especially during the winter, the monks could pursue the more artistic labors of academic study, particularly music. They began to interpret and translate musical manuscripts, and make copies of them. The monks sang in plainsong (see page 14) at most of their church services and were fundamental in the development of music over the following centuries.

Above: By the Middle Ages music was still centered around religion. In the 13th century composers in France began to write songs for three voices—which could either be religious, as depicted here, or nonchurch.

the book of Exodus and is associated with the Day of Judgment. But the most famous mention of the *shofar* is when the seven priests played them and brought down the walls of Jericho.

Incantation

It is also written in the Bible that Jesus and his disciples sang **hymns** and **psalms**. Hymns were considered to be the songs of angels, while psalms were the songs of men. Early Christians were also aware of the power of both melody and words, spoken or sung in a repetitive way, to inspire awe and well-being in the listener and create a religious atmosphere. This type of spoken singing is called **incantation**. Music came to be considered a natural

element to be added to the practice of Christian worship.

During the first 200 years of the Christian church Christians were few in number and often persecuted. The development of church music, therefore, was not a high priority. By the early years of the third century, however, church numbers had grown, and music that was suitable for worship became more sought after.

The early church wanted to break away from the music used in pre-Christian festivals. The ancient Romans had inherited the Greek love of music for their festivals, and by association this music was therefore considered entirely inappropriate for the church. Also, dancing was associated with this music, and dancing was thought to be entirely unsuitable behavior for Christians. This is why rhythm, which creates the urge to dance, was discouraged as an element of church music. Even the use of instruments was considered improper, with the result that singing in the Christian church remained unaccompanied by instruments for the first 1,000 years of its existence.

It is not known where the early church got its first music. Music was not written down by the Christians, even in its crudest form, until the sixth century A.D. At least some of it must have had its origins in Greek and Jewish music. Greek was the language of the early church, and melodies were passed down orally. However, this was an inaccurate method of passing on very detailed information, and such music is therefore most likely to have changed considerably over many years.

Gregorian chant

The form of the Christian church service and its music was standardized by Pope Gregory I (*c*.540–604). In honor of him the unaccompanied melodies of the church service are now referred to as Gregorian chant. This music is also called plainchant or plainsong. The music uses a free rhythm, just as if the words were being spoken instead of sung. The chants, always sung in Latin, use the natural rhythm and stresses of the words. It also uses a system of scales called modes, which was originally invented by Pythagoras (see page 10).

Gregorian chant has survived to the present day in almost the same form as when it was first created. From the ninth to the 12th centuries, however, composers—at this time mostly monks in the monasteries—began to experiment

with and add their own new melodies and texts to the catalog of those already existing. They also began to combine, in a single **piece** of music, both traditional melodies and new melodies, which resulted in an entirely new style of music. This new style of music was called **organum** (see the example on page 21). The word organum is Latin for "instrument," although it is not known for sure why the term was used to define this type of music.

Above: A painting (*c*.1620) of Pope Gregory. It is in his honor that early Christian church music is referred to as Gregorian chant.

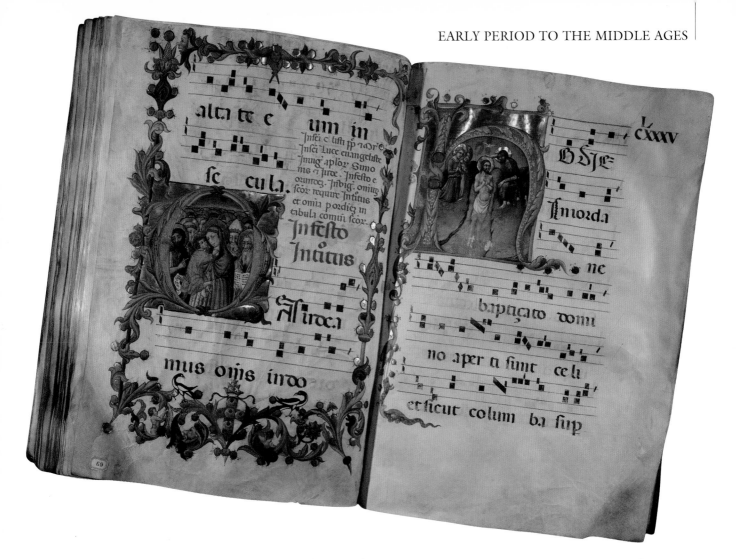

Above: Pius II's illuminated *Book of Psalms,* showing written notes for a Gregorian chant.

The beginnings of polyphony

The composers of organum would take a previously existing melody and then add the same melody to it, but at a higher or lower pitch (see the example on page 21). These second melodies were either written an octave apart (eight notes higher or lower) or a fourth or fifth interval apart (four or five notes higher or lower). Later, composers began to give the plainchant melody to a low voice, which they called the **tenor**. The words were sung in long, slow notes, while a second voice elaborated the melody in shorter notes above it. This added melody was known as a clausula (meaning "to close" or "to conclude" in Latin). The Christian church approved of this new style of composition as long as the musical elaborations did not take away from the meaning of the holy words.

Music was now made up of more than one melody. The new style came to be called **polyphony**. This word means "many voices" (or **parts**) and comes from the Greek *polu* meaning "many" and *phone* meaning "voice."

The first important school of polyphonic composers originated in Paris, France. One of the greatest of these organum composers was Léonin (*c.*1163–1190). He wrote a large collection of two-voiced polyphony known as the *Magnus Liber* ("big book") for Notre Dame Cathedral in Paris, where he worked.

Léonin's work was continued by his compatriot Pérotin (born *c.*1200). As well as composing works in the new polyphonic style, Pérotin made important advances in musical **notation**, which is the system of writing down music for others to learn and perform.

15

The first musical notation

It was a French Benedictine monk, Guido d'Arezzo (*c*.955–1050) who developed a system of **sight singing** that—in its slightly more modernized form of *doh, re, mi, fa, sol, la, ti, doh*—is still in use today. It helped singers learn new chants more easily and within a very short period of time. An important part of this system was a technique for writing down music. This technique used lines and spaces, with high notes placed at the top and low notes at the bottom.

In about 1025 Guido moved from Ferrara, Italy—where he had been educated and created his innovative system—to Arezzo, Italy. It was here that he was invited to demonstrate his new idea to the Pope. He set out his new system in his book *Micrologus*, together with his commentary on other music of his day. It became one of the most copied and studied instruction books on music in the Middle Ages and enabled singers anywhere to read, learn, and sing the same songs.

Below: Guido d'Arezzo developed a system of writing music that he was able to teach to others. In this way it became possible for people to write, read, and learn music more quickly.

The motet

In the early 13th century composers in France began to add words to the decorated upper part (the clausula) of the plainsong. This idea soon grew into an independent composition, and a new name was coined for it—the **motet**. The motet was almost always written for three voices: the lower tenor voice was always the plainsong, the middle voice was known as the

---

The words of a motet could be either religious or secular

---

duplum, and the upper voice as the triplum. The words could be either religious or **secular** (nonchurch); if secular, the words were often those of a well-known popular song.

The French composer Philippe de Vitry (1291–1361) was a poet, composer, and music theorist. The title of his book *Ars nova* (the "new art") is now used to describe all the music of the 14th century. The book includes much comment on the notation and rhythm of the period. De Vitry became a master of motet composition. In his works can be seen some of the earliest applications of **time signatures**, which are signs placed at the beginning of a piece of music to indicate its basic rhythm.

The French composer Guillaume de Machaut (*c*.1300–1377) was greatly influenced by De Vitry's *Ars nova* and used many of its guidelines in his music. As well as writing a large number of motets, he wrote a famous piece of uplifting ceremonial music in 1364 for the coronation of Charles V of France.

Minstrels

Although musical history in the Middle Ages centered around the church, nonchurch music also flourished at this time. However, less written evidence of this secular music has survived.

Much of the nonchurch, or secular, music of the Middle Ages was performed by minstrels, who were professional (paid) entertainers from medieval times up until the 17th century. Minstrels were either self-employed or permanently attached to a household or court, where they played at weddings, celebrations, and court events. Self-employed minstrels wandered from town to town and village to village—anywhere they thought work could be found. In France minstrels were called jongleurs (literally "jugglers"). They not only had to be good with their hands but were also expected to play several instruments, do acrobatics, perform tricks (often with trained animals), and provide a range of other types of entertainment. Each year during Lent (the six weeks before Easter) they held an annual gathering where they learned new songs and tricks.

The earliest surviving songs from this period are in Latin and date from the 11th and 12th centuries. Directed at educated audiences, the songs were sung by goliards—minstrels who were scholars and men of the church, and who were also often teachers.

Although the goliards' songs were secular, they often included moral or religious meanings within them. In Germany wandering minstrels were known as minnesingers. The lyrics of their songs told of knights and courtly love, the accepted behavior and expression of love between men and women in the courts at that time. In the 14th and early 15th centuries gatherings of European minstrels were held in the Netherlands and at Beauvais in France every year.

Troubadours

In Provence, southern France, a more elite group of minstrels developed called troubadours. Troubadours were wandering singers who wrote poetry in their local language, Provençal, which they then set to music as songs to perform. The word "troubadour" originally meant a writer or a poet.

Troubadours performed in the royal courts, so it was important for them to be well skilled in their art. In northern France, where the songs of the troubadours became popular later on, they were known as trouvères.

Many troubadour songs have survived to this day. However, since

COMPETITIVE MUSIC FESTIVALS IN BRITAIN AND FRANCE

Competitive festivals have had an important place in Western European culture for over 2,500 years. The first competitive festivals in the British Isles took place in Wales. They were called *eisteddfods*, a Welsh word meaning "assembly" or "session." The first recorded *eisteddfod* took place in Cardigan, Wales, in 1176, but it is likely that other gatherings took place long before this date. The *eisteddfods* centered around competitions in music and literature, and were gatherings for musician-poets called bards. Bards were paid by local kings, princes, and chieftains, and their duties were to compose poetry and music and to sing songs, usually accompanying themselves with a harp. As competitive music festivals *eisteddfods* have survived in Wales until the present day.

In northern France literary and musical societies called *puys* held contests for singers from about the 12th century. The competitors sang lyrical songs called chansons. The singer of the best song was crowned and rewarded, and given the title *prince du puy*. Puys existed in many of the major cities of northern France and even in London, England. These societies were active until the 17th century.

Left: This painting shows a medieval minstrel with a lute entertaining a group of people with songs of courtly love.

there is often no indication of rhythm, it is difficult for modern interpreters to know exactly how the songs would have been sung. Songs vary from the very simple to the more complex **ballad**, which may have several characters involved in it. Some songs called for dancing and mime, and the **chorus** section often called for several singers. Many songs show the influence of Gregorian chant, while in turn, the songs of the troubadours influenced the French secular motet.

The traditions of the minstrels and the troubadours were lost by the 17th century. The courtly troubadours, essentially an oral tradition, are said to have disappeared with the arrival of written music as their songs became more available to others through musical notation. Meanwhile, minstrels—who traveled to perform

at fairs, weddings, and festivals—
were often poor and homeless, traits
that eventually led to them being
discouraged and treated as outsiders
by local communities.

Music on the move

However, it was the troubadours and
minstrels who carried many of the
musical ideas that took root in the
next century. Their traveling lifestyle
helped distribute new musical ideas
and forms from one country to the
next all the way across Europe. This
cross-fertilization of different musical
styles created a more international

Right: A troubadour
plays at an outdoor
entertainment
for members of
the court in this
illuminated medieval
manuscript from the
late 13th century.

music and paved the way for many of
the developments and innovations
that appeared in the next musical
era—that of the Renaissance.

Left: Musicians can
be seen playing a
variety of medieval
instruments in this
German painting from
1520. An early form
of musical notation
can be seen on the
banner above the
musicians' heads.

INSTRUMENTS IN THE MIDDLE AGES

Present-day knowledge about what type of instruments
existed in the Middle Ages originates primarily from art.
Almost every artist's portrayal of a celebration or similar
social occasion of the period shows a group or groups of
instrumentalists. Many of the elaborate book illustrations
made by monks also regularly feature instruments.
There are also references to instruments in much of the
poetry from this period.

    The musicians of the Middle Ages had a relatively large
and varied selection of instruments available to them. The

harp dates from before the ninth century. The *vielle* ("fiddle"
in England) was an early bowed instrument popular with
minstrels and was the predecessor of the violin. The
organistrum was a stringed instrument operated by a
revolving wheel, which later developed into the well-known
hurdy-gurdy. There were flutes and shawms (early oboes),
and trumpets and horns. Apart from the church organ there
were also portable organs. Drums entered the musical scene
quite late in the 12th century and were immediately taken
up as rhythm keepers in dance music.

CHAPTER 2

A Rebirth

The Renaissance marked a revival of interest in ancient Greece and Rome, as well as a growing interest in new ideas and cultures. With one foot in the past, music marched into the future.

The word *renaissance* is French for "rebirth." The term is used to describe the period from the 15th to 16th centuries when ancient Greek and Roman art had an important influence on the art, architecture, and sculpture of the time. Many ancient artworks were discovered during these years, which increased interest in the ancient world even further. The artists of the Renaissance saw their works as a reblossoming of the glories of Greece and Rome.

In music, unlike art, no Greek or Roman works survive; but ancient writings of music theorists were preserved, and Renaissance composers used their ideas in their own works. They learned, for example, that ancient music used monody (one **melody**) rather than **harmony**—two or more musical **notes** sounding together in a "harmonious," or complementary, way. By the end of the Renaissance the rediscovery of the monodic song led to a new art form

Above: The painting *Pierides Challenge Muses in Song and Change into Magpies* by the 16th-century Italian artist Jacopo Tintoretto is just one of the many examples of a Renaissance artist choosing a subject from ancient Greece for his work.

Sit glo - ri - a Do - mi - ni, in sae - cu - la lae - ta - bi - tur Do - mi - nus in o - pe - ri - bus su - is.

Above: In this example of parallel organum the main plainsong melody is seen in the top line of notes. Underneath it is a second part that repeats the melody in fifth intervals.

based around a strong single melody—opera (see pages 32–33).

Renaissance composers also used the Greek system of **scales**—called **modes**—as the basis of their music (see page 10). Yet by the end of the 16th century they found that this modal system could not express the range of emotion or musical colors they required, so they became more interested in the use of harmony.

The development of harmony

The music of ancient Greece did not have harmony in the way the word is used today. To them harmony was the relationship between ongoing notes of a melody. Different notes were not sounded together, and instruments and voices played and sang the same melody. Ancient harmony was based entirely on the melody, meaning that each note in the melody influenced the notes that came before or after it.

In other words, imagine that notes in a melody are like stepping stones in a stream, and you want to cross from one side of the stream to the other. The stone you step on next depends on where it is in relation to the one you are standing on at the moment, and you will choose the stones that will help you get to the other side of the stream in the best possible way. A composer will also choose the notes that complete the melody in the best way. The pattern that your steps form, moving from one stone to the next, could be seen as the melody line. Since you are "crossing" the stream, your steps are moving in a generally horizontal direction. Therefore melody can be seen as a horizontal movement of notes.

Harmony as it is now known—that is, two or more notes sounding together—began in the Middle Ages as a development of the plainsong (see page 14). The plainsong melody was accompanied by one or more additional **parts**—lines of music sung by a singer or played by a musician. The parts moved parallel to each other in what was called **organum**. Parts were added to the plainsong melody in **intervals**—the distances between the notes—of fourths, fifths, or **octaves** either above or below the melody (see example above).

In the Middle Ages composers tended to use only the intervals of the fourth, fifth, and octave—called **consonances**, since these were considered to sound the "strongest." However, many composers began to rebel against this strictness and to use other intervals. English composers began to use the third interval to increase the variety of the harmony. By the late 13th century composers were using mostly third and sixth intervals to build their melodies. Later, England led Europe again in allowing the two parts to "cross over," so that the low part became the higher part at times, while the high part became the lower part. In this way new harmonies were created.

The dawn of modern harmony

A system of harmony more like the one composers use today began in France and Italy in the 14th century. It came about gradually, as composers abandoned the idea of building harmony with parallel parts moving in a horizontal relationship to each other and began to view harmony as a

21

"vertical" relationship between the musical parts (see examples below).

This change in the way composers wrote harmony was influenced by the development of musical instruments. Many early musical instruments—such as the voice, flute, recorder, trumpet,

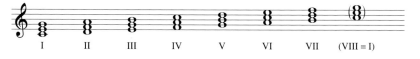

I   II   III   IV   V   VI   VII   (VIII = I)

and was combined with the fifth interval to form a triad—a three-note chord made up of the first note of the scale along with its third and fifth intervals. The triad chord can be built on every note of the scale and has now become the basis of modern harmony.

Above: These are triad chords based on the C scale—the scale beginning with C and ending on the C an octave above. Each triad chord consists of three notes: the first note, the third interval above, and the fifth interval above. The chords move upward from the first C chord to the next C chord.

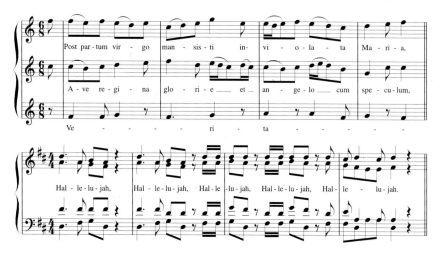

Above: In horizontal harmony (top example) the upper main melody is mirrored by the other parts using either the same notes or notes in strict intervals. In vertical harmony (bottom example) the parts are made up of different notes that are layered in a vertical relationship called chords.

or horn—could only sing or play one melody line, or one part, at a time. Yet as instrument making progressed, instruments such as the lute and the keyboard were invented that were able to play more than one note, and therefore more than one part, at the same time. Composers then began to write works in which a single instrument played more than one part. This resulted in the development of the **chord**—three or more notes from the same scale that are sounded together. Chords are built by notes placed one on top of the other. The relationship between the notes is therefore vertical, and this type of harmony is called vertical harmony.

By the mid-15th century the third interval was used to build harmony

Accepting vertical harmony

The new harmony was set out in the book *Le istitutioni harmoniche* ("The Institution of Harmony"), published in 1558 by the Italian composer and music theorist Gioseffo Zarlino (*c*.1517–1590). He stressed the advantage of chords, the triad system, and the cadence—a way of ending a musical phrase, section, or work. At this time composers also began to use progressions—moving from one note to another, or from one chord to another, in a regular pattern (see example at top of page). Individual parts were still decorated as they were in **polyphonic** music (see page 15), but by the end of the 16th century vertical harmony became accepted as a basic element of music.

The view of harmony as vertical chords was one of the biggest revolutions in music and had a great influence on the way music was composed.

Below and below right: A painting of the music theorist Gioseffo Zarlino and the title page of his important book "The Institution of Harmony."

THE FIRST PRINTED MUSIC

Guido d'Arrezo had created a method of writing down music in the 11th century and invented staves—the lines and spaces on which musical notes are written. But as music compositions became more popular, and more detailed, it was necessary to copy them down faster and in larger numbers since copying them by hand was slow and difficult.

However, the printing of music was a more complex process than the printing of words because it used signs and symbols rather than just words. Music printing therefore developed more slowly. The first printed music books were of plainsong and were printed in Rome, Italy, in 1476. In 1501 the Italian printer Ottaviano dei Petrucci (1466–1539) published the first books of polyphonic music. In these early publications the staves were printed in red ink, using wood blocks, and the notes were then printed over them in black. The notes were diamond-shaped or square, with stems attached to the center of the note. The slanted oval shape that is used in music notes today did not become established until the late 17th century.

The invention of music printing was important in the development of music. It was no longer necessary for music manuscripts to be copied by hand, or for plainsong to be passed down by one priest singing to another.

Above: A page from *Collection canti B numero 50*—one of Ottaviano dei Petrucci's first printed music books.

It is perhaps something like the difference between a color photograph and a black-and-white photograph. If you had never seen a color photograph before, you would be satisfied with a black-and-white photograph since it still showed many characteristics and details, and you would probably not feel that anything was missing. But if you were to then see a color photograph, you would see other elements in the photograph that you had not thought about before. It could be said that the new harmony brought more "color" into the music.

Music's role in Renaissance life

The Renaissance was a time of exploration and discovery. Columbus was crossing the boundary of the Atlantic Ocean to "discover" the Americas, while scientists and astronomers were crossing new boundaries of thought to discover things about the world and the solar system. Not only were new ideas spreading from one country to another, but they were also being passed on more easily between people in the same society. Learning and education became very important, universities thrived, and every nobleman's son had a tutor who taught him Latin, the sciences, and the arts—including music. Therefore, people who could teach music were needed in many homes of the wealthy.

Musicians were also needed by the church since by this time music was an essential part of the church service. Most monks were expected to be able to sing, and music became important in their education. These monks formed **choirs**—organized groups of singers—that sang in Latin during the church services. As the Renaissance continued, choirs became bigger and bigger, and needed to be directed. The role of the **conductor**—a person

Above: This engraving from 1475 shows three students being tutored in singing.

who directs the performers by making gestures that mark the time and the **rhythm** of the music—came into practice at this point. Posts became available in many churches for choir conductors and music directors to organize the music at each church service. This led to the church becoming one of the greatest patrons of music in the Renaissance.

By the 16th century the Lutheran church—the German Protestant church led by Martin Luther—decided to include the entire church congregation in the singing of the church service because it was felt that this would bring people closer to God. Since many of them did not speak Latin, composers began to write **hymns** in German to be sung by the congregation after the choir had sung. In this way, common people began to participate in the music of the church.

Another place where music flourished during the Renaissance was in the royal courts. The courts would hire musicians, often called minstrels, to entertain the guests of royalty with singing, usually accompanied by an instrument. Such entertainment caused a greater interest in the **secular** (nonchurch) song, which soon became very popular.

The chanson

The first French secular song was the chanson, which simply means "song" in French. From the chanson, more complex compositions were written that included several voices. The composer Guillaume de Machaut (*c*.1300–1377) did the most to develop the chanson and to introduce a more modern sense of harmony. He favored the third and sixth intervals rather than the traditional intervals of the fifth and octave.

The first major group of chanson writers emerged around northern France, Belgium, and Holland in the 15th century. Its composers are now often referred to as belonging to the "Burgundian" school after the

---

The lyrics of the chansons were usually about love and the customs of the knights

---

wealthy and influential court of Burgundy that attracted many of the great musicians of the time. Its leading composers were Guillaume Dufay (*c*.1398–1474) and Gilles de Bins dit Binchois (*c*.1400–1460), who both developed the chanson style in their own ways. Their music is now considered equally important, although Dufay was more famous at the time. He was very influenced by the English composer John Dunstable (1370–1453). The **lyrics** of these chansons usually spoke of love and chivalry (the customs of knights).

The anthem

The English version of the chanson was the **anthem**. It is a short song written in English with moral or religious lyrics and a powerful **chorus**. At this time the chorus was the

Right: Two of the greatest writers of chansons from the Burgundian school—Guillaume Dufay, standing in front of an organ, and Gilles de Bins dit Binchois, leaning on a harp. They are shown discussing music together in this 15th-century manuscript.

section of the composition sung by the choir. There are two types of anthems: the full anthem, which is sung by a choir throughout, usually without any accompaniment, and the verse anthem. The verse anthem starts with a verse sung by a soloist and accompanied by an instrument that is followed by a chorus sung by a choir. In a verse anthem the pattern of verse and then chorus could be repeated a number of times.

Below: A painting of Thomas Tallis, one of the first composers of the anthem.

The first anthems were written for the church. A pioneer of the anthem was the composer and organist Thomas Tallis (c.1505–1585). His best-known work is the **motet** *Spem in alium* (c.1560), also known as "Sing and Glorify," which was written for eight choirs singing five parts each. It was probably intended to be performed with each choir

located in a different part of the church. Tallis wrote many of his anthems by translating vocal sections from his Latin motets into English. They were then published separately. His work influenced other composers such as William Byrd (1543–1623) and Thomas Morley (1557–1603). Byrd's "Sing Joyfully" and Morley's "Out of the Deep," both written in 1641, are good, lively examples of early anthems.

English composers continued to develop the style of the anthem, and some 200 years later it crossed the Atlantic, inspiring the great anthems of North America in the 18th century.

The madrigal

While the English were developing the anthem and the French were writing chansons, the Italians were composing songs in a similar style, which they called madrigals. The earliest were written in about 1320 and had two or three musical parts, with the upper part being the more elaborate. The blind composer Francesco Landini (c.1325–1397) wrote about 140 compositions called ballates, which were an early form of the madrigal.

The great Italian madrigal of the 16th century came from the *frottola*—a light polyphonic song in three or four parts. The lyrics of *frottolas* were written in a simple form and were usually funny and carefree. The music did not try to express the words. Madrigal lyrics, on the other hand, expressed more serious emotions and were written in free form—without a set rhythm. The music of the madrigal used imitation—one part echoing the melody of another—and word-painting, such as the word "running" set to a flurry of quick notes, or a

MADRIGALS IN ENGLAND

The English madrigal was slow to develop; but when it did, it inspired some of the most important madrigals of the late 16th century. One reason for its slow growth was that English poetry at the time was not suited to the madrigal style. Yet the Italian madrigal soon became popular in England, and the English singer and music editor Nicholas Yonge (1561–1619) published *Musica Transalpina*—a collection of Italian

madrigals translated into English—in 1588. By this time a change had occurred in English poetry—the rise of the sonnet. The sonnet was a poem of 14 lines with a formal rhyming pattern that suited the madrigal perfectly. When used for lyrics, the form of the sonnet was **improvised** on so it became looser. Many of the great anthem composers began to write madrigals, and in 1588 William Byrd wrote "Though Amaryliss Dance in Green," the first English madrigal.

The title "madrigal" was used in England for the first time in 1594, in a collection by Thomas Morley, a pupil of Byrd. Morley became the leader of the English madrigal school and edited a book of 23 madrigals called *The Triumphes of Oriana* (1601), written by the best English madrigal composers of the day. He dedicated the book to Queen Elizabeth I. Each madrigal ends with the words "Long live fair Oriana"—the name used for Elizabeth I by poets of the time. The book included two madrigals by Morley, one of which, "Hard by a Crystal Fountain," is among his best works.

Left: This 16th-century painting is thought to be of Elizabeth I dancing at court with the Earl of Leicester.

melancholy-sounding collection of notes on a word like "woe."

The Flemish composer Adrian Willaert (1490–1562) was one of the first composers of the Italian madrigal. He lived, composed, and taught in Venice, Italy, for most of his life and wrote over 70 madrigals, published from 1536. At the height of the madrigal's popularity its most famous Italian composers were Andrea Gabrieli (see page 30), Giovanni Pierluigi da Palestrina (see pages 28–29), and Orlando di Lasso (see page 29).

Madrigals were usually written for unaccompanied voices, but composers often headed their manuscripts "for voices or instruments." This gave rise to a number of different madrigal **arrangements**—musical compositions rewritten for different instruments. Most of these arrangements were for

the lute because it suited the nature of the music. Therefore the madrigal led to some of the earliest lute music.

The lute

The lute made its way into European culture from the Arab world—where it was called the oud, the Arabic word for wood— when the Moors conquered Spain in the late Middle Ages. It is a stringed instrument with a wooden body shaped like a pear half. By the 16th and 17th centuries it had became one of the most popular solo and accompanying instruments in the Western world.

No lutes made before the 16th century have survived. It is therefore difficult for people today to know

Below and below right: A lute made in 1621 in Basel, Switzerland, and a 15th-century painting by the Italian artist Lorenzo Costa called *A Concert*, showing a lutenist performing with two singers.

how these lutes were constructed or what they looked like. However, they do know that lute strings were tuned in pairs, with two strings sounding the same note, and that the lutes were built in many different sizes. This pairing of the strings increased the loudness of the instrument.

The lute was first played with a **pick**, as it still is today in the Arab world. In the 15th century, however, it became the Western fashion to play the lute with the fingers. This allowed players to sound up to four notes at the same time, which was a distinct advantage for playing chords and caused a new skill to develop—playing in four parts. At roughly the same time, a system for writing lute music developed. It was called tablature and used letters, numbers, and various signs instead of traditional **notation**.

Composers for the lute

The lute was one of the most fashionable instruments in Europe until the 18th century. During its peak in the 16th century it was used

Above: The *First Booke of Songes or Ayres*, written by John Dowland in 1597, shows some of the signs and letters that were used in tablature—a system of music notation used for lute music of the time.

both in the home and in public to accompany singing. Because of its popularity it gave rise to a large number of lute players, called lutenists, and lutenist-composers.

In England the lutenist-composer John Dowland (1563–1626) published his *First Booke of Songes or Ayres of Foure Partes with Tableture for Lute* in 1597. Three similar books followed. Together these four books formed the most important collection of English solo songs with lute accompaniment. Dowland traveled all over Europe during his lifetime. He took his first lutenist's job in Paris at the age of 17, where he soon gained a reputation both as a composer and performer. His lifelong ambition was to be a lutenist at the English royal court, but he only achieved this at the very end of his life.

In Italy lute music spread quickly thanks to Petrucci's printing press in Venice. The composer Vincenzo Capirola (*c.*1474–1550) wrote the most important Italian lute music of the early 16th century and impressed King Henry VIII of England on a visit in 1515. Soon afterward,

Francesco Canova da Milano (1497–1543) achieved international fame for his lute compositions.

The church organ

Like the lute, the church organ was used to accompany the human voice. The first organ was invented by the Greek engineer Ktesibios in about 300 B.C. in Alexandria, Egypt. The Greeks called it the *hydraulos*. It had a loud, piercing **tone**—sound quality— and water was used to control the air pressure (in Greek *hydro* means "water" and *aulos* means "pipe").

It is probably because the hydraulis was commonly used for non-Christian rites that it was never accepted by the Christian church. From the ninth century the Church organ was pneumatic (*pneuma* is Greek for "breath"), meaning that it worked by air being pumped through bellows. A keyboard was not added until the 13th century. Before then notes were sounded by a series of "slides" that were pushed in and out (see the example below). The organ that was built in the cathedral at Winchester,

England, in 950 A.D. was extremely large. A description of the day reports that it had 400 pipes and 26 bellows, and was worked by 70 men!

By the early Renaissance organs had been built in most of the large cathedrals. New features were added to the organ, and its tone began to change. By 1500 most organs in France, England, and northern Italy still had one keyboard and about 10 stops—knobs that control the flow of air to the different organ pipes (see the example below right). Stops can also change the tone of a note. Meanwhile some German organs, the most advanced in Europe, had two or three keyboards. The pedal board (a row of foot pedals) was also invented in Germany in the mid-15th century. The organ of today was more or less fully developed by the 17th century.

Master of organ music

One of the leading composers for the organ in the early Renaissance was Giovanni Pierluigi da Palestrina (1525–1594). His first position was as an organist and choirmaster in the cathedral of Palestrina, near Rome.

Apart from over 140 madrigals— written in a traditional style that he later dismissed as antireligious—and some keyboard works, Palestrina's music was written for the church. Of his 104 masses his most famous

Above: This 16th-century organ in Roskilde Cathedral in Denmark shows the elaborate detail and decoration that were striking features of organs during the Renaissance period.

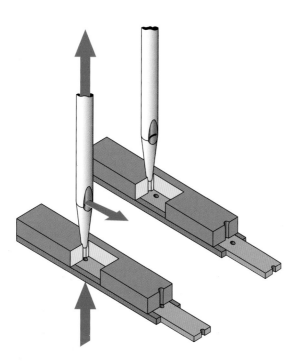

Left: Slides are used to sound notes in some organs. Only when a hole in the slide is aligned with the pipe above it (as in the example at left) will the air sound through the pipe.

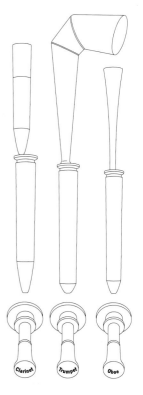

Right: From 1500, stops, controlled by knobs, were used to change the tone of a note.

Above: The great Italian composer Giovanni Pierluigi da Palestrina plays the organ during a choral rehearsal.

were *Missa Papae Marcelli* and *Missa Assumpta est Maria*, both written in 1567. Most of his masses are based on Gregorian chant (see page 14). He also wrote 375 motets and 68 offertories—works played during the service while the priest prepared the bread and wine for the offering.

Palestrina's style of harmony was influenced by composers who came before him and lived in Rome, but he was never affected by the harmonic experiments of the more revolutionary composers of his own time, such as Carlo Gesualdo (see page 30). Palestrina studied the works of the Franco-Flemish composers and adopted their polyphonic techniques.

Franco-Flemish school

The Roman school of polyphony that Palestrina was a part of had its roots in the Franco-Flemish school.

Between 1450 and 1550 most of the important music posts in Europe were held by composers who were from an area between northern France and Amsterdam, Holland. These composers have therefore come to be known as the Franco-Flemish school. The first composer of the Franco-Flemish school was

Below: An engraving of the French composer Josquin des Prés, who became a singer at Milan Cathedral and one of the most influential composers of the Renaissance.

Johannes Ockeghem (*c*.1410–1497), who taught many of its later composers. Ockeghem wrote fewer compositions than many of the other composers from this school, yet he was greatly respected, and his death inspired several lamentations—works expressing sadness at the death of a fellow composer.

Josquin des Prés (*c*.1440–1521), who may have been a pupil of Ockeghem, was one of the most influential Renaissance composers. He was considered a master of melody and composition, and left behind more works that still survive than any other composer of his time. Even after his death he was so respected that his works were continually reprinted. A French chanson, "*L'homme armé*," that des Prés used in one of his first masses became so popular that it was used in more than 30 compositions written by other important composers of the time such as Ockeghem, Dufay, and Palestrina.

One of the last composers of the Franco-Flemish school was Orlando di Lasso (1532–1594). Born in Mons, Belgium, he went to Italy at an early age and later to Munich, Germany, where he stayed for almost 40 years until he died. He was a very adaptable composer, writing in all the musical forms of his day, and managed to write more than 2,000 compositions.

Lasso's greatest work is considered to be *The Seven Penitential Psalms of David*, published in 1584. In this motet he uses *musica reservata*—a style of composition in which the words are given special attention to make sure that their meaning is reflected in the music. This style was very popular with the court. The composer's employer at Munich, Duke Albrecht V, paid Lasso to write this work and was later so impressed with the music that

CARLO GESUALDO— RENAISSANCE INNOVATOR

The Italian composer and nobleman Carlo Gesualdo (1560–1613) was one of the most revolutionary composers of the Renaissance. In his 100 madrigals he tried to mirror the mood of the lyrics in the music. For instance, to express sad or painful emotions, he used dissonance—two or more notes that create a tension or discomfort in the listener when sounded together— far more freely in his music than other composers of his time. The result is music of high drama and great emotional expression. To

Above: Carlo Gesualdo kneels beside his uncle Carlo Borromeo in a Renaissance painting.

achieve this, he abandoned the rules and conventions of his day, and introduced **chromatic** harmony, which moved quickly through changes of **key** (the central note that the composition is based around) in the 12-**semitone** scale (see page 11). He also used daring **modulations**— sequences of changes that ease the listener into the next key. In his use of these musical techniques he was truly a prophet of the future.

Gesualdo was interested in music and poetry as a young man, and became an excellent performer on the archlute, a large **bass** lute. He was rich enough to be able to hide away from the rest of society in his estate outside Naples and spend his days writing music. It is thought that his isolation from the world allowed him to be more adventuresome in his use of musical ideas and techniques than other composers, who were more dependent on other people's approval.

he had the manuscript copied and illustrated by the court painter, and bound in two handsome volumes.

Music at St. Marks, Venice

Many composers of the Franco-Flemish school took up positions in Italy, where the centers of musical excellence were Naples, Florence, Ferrara, Modena, Mantua, Milan, and Venice. During the early years of the Renaissance Venice was Italy's musical capital. St. Mark's, its great 11th-century cathedral, formed the hub of Venetian musical culture. All state ceremonies took place inside the building or on the piazza in front.

Adrian Willaert was made *Maestro di Cappella* (music director) at St. Mark's in 1527—the most desirable musical post in Italy. Although he was born in Bruges, Belgium, he came to Italy in 1522. At St. Mark's there were two organs and two choirs, and Willaert set about using them in his music. Both the choirs and the organs were in separate galleries on opposite sides of the church—a feature that he used to create echo effects. At times he used the two choirs together, which produced a very powerful result. One of his pupils, Andrea Gabrieli (1520–1586), later became second organist at St. Mark's. Gabrieli added his own **antiphonal** music, in which the performers are in separated groups, to that created by Willaert.

Reaching a peak of sound

With Giovanni Gabrieli (*c*.1553-1612), Andrea's nephew and pupil, came the peak of late Renaissance and early Baroque music at St. Mark's. His *Sonata pian e forte*, composed in 1597, is one of the first works to use **dynamics**—markings such as louds and softs on written music that tell the musician how a note or musical phrase should be played. It is also one of the first works to give precise **orchestration**, in which the composer assigns a specific instrument to a specific musical part. The first instrumental group called for is three trombones and a cornett—a wind instrument made of wood with finger-holes and a cup-shaped mouthpiece. The second group of instruments asks

Above: In this 16th-century painting of St. Mark's Square, Venice, a ceremony is taking place in front of the famous St. Mark's Cathedral. Music would have been an important part of the ceremony.

for three trombones and viol—a stringed instrument resembling the violin that is held on the lap or between the instrumentalist's legs and played with a bow. Giovanni used all the singers and musicians that were made available to him: his work *Omnes gentes* (1597) was written for four choirs, strings, and wind instruments.

The Renaissance motet

The large choirs and orchestras available to church composers such as the two Gabrielis led to a new style of motet by the second half of the 16th century. During the early Renaissance the motet had been a composition for unaccompanied voices. The text, in Latin, still used an existing plainsong melody as the lower vocal part (the **tenor**) and different texts for the two upper parts. This plainsong, when it formed the basis of a polyphonic composition, was called the cantus firmus (Latin for "fixed melody") because it stayed the same throughout the work. The cantus firmus often consisted of long-sounding notes, while the other parts were composed using shorter-sounding notes. Cantus firmus was used in both vocal and instrumental polyphonic works.

After 1500, however, the plainsong melody was abandoned, and the motet became entirely original music, with all the parts set to the same text. The composers of the Franco-Flemish school were

largely responsible for this musical development. Their compositions were in a polyphonic style for four to six parts and used a lot of imitation. They also had some homophonic sections in which the voices sang the same basic rhythm in harmony based on the chords. The words became increasingly important as composers tried to develop a closeness between the words of the text and the expression in the music.

By the end of the Renaissance era composers like the Gabrielis had taken the motet to new heights. They used two or more choirs in antiphonal style to repeat a verse or **psalm** and so reinforce its meaning. Motets from the late Renaissance were often accompanied by an orchestra of many types of instruments. As the motet continued to develop, it paved the way for the vocal **cantata**—the most important form of church music composed during the Baroque era that was about to dawn.

Right: The great Flemish composer Orlando di Lasso stands on the left in front of the choir at the Chapel Royal in Munich, Germany.

CHAPTER 3

A Misshapen Pearl

The word "baroque" has been used since the 20th century to describe the era of European music from about 1600 to 1750. The era began with the first operas ever written and reached a climax with the works of Bach and Handel.

The word Baroque comes from the Portuguese word *barroco*, meaning a "misshapen pearl." The term was originally used to describe the grotesque, distorted, and extravagant. By the 19th century it was used to define any highly decorated art, including painting, sculpture, and architecture. Finally, the word was applied to music. Since the 20th century it has been used to refer to the period in European music history from about 1600 to 1750. The works of Bach and Handel, which bring the era to a close, are thought to be the high points of Baroque music.

Baroque composers used a number of methods and practices, called conventions, in their music. One such convention was for composers to create huge contrasts in the music by changing the **tempo**—the speed at

Above: A "grotesque, distorted, and extravagant" statue from the Baroque era.

which musical **notes** are played—from slow to fast. Contrast was also created by **dynamics**, such as playing loudly and then softly. Another convention that Baroque composers used was the basso continuo **part**—the "continuous **bass**" line that ran throughout the entire composition. The basso continuo part contained the lowest notes of the **chords** on which Baroque composers built their **harmonies**.

Another Baroque stylistic practice was the "doctrine of the affections" (see box opposite). The **melody**, especially the vocal part, was highly decorated with musical ornaments (see top of page 33). The decoration was often **improvised** by the singers or musicians. In Baroque opera (stage plays set to music), the performers used certain elegant "gestures" when moving on the stage.

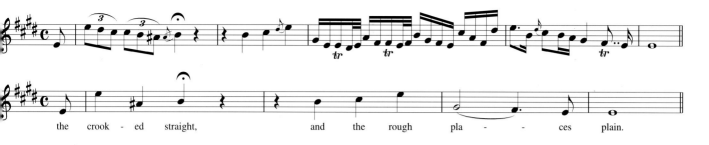

the crook - ed straight, and the rough pla - - ces plain.

The first operas

The first musical dramas were known as *intermedi* (Italian for "in the middle") because they were short works performed in between the acts or "in the middle" of plays or other grand entertainments. They were used as a light relief from the more serious emotions of the main play. *Intermedi* were usually about love and country life or based on classical mythology, and included recitative (speech that was sung), song, and ballet—the disciplined dance form accompanied by music and performed on a stage that was invented around this time.

As *intermedi* became increasingly popular with audiences, they became

Above: The top example shows a decorated melody from the Baroque era. The example below it shows the same melody without decoration, or ornamentation. In a decorated melody notes were added, and signs indicated the specific type of decoration called for. The sign *tr* called for a trill—the main note wavering up a tone or semitone in pitch.

a more important part of the entertainment, until eventually they were performed as works in their own right and called operas (the word "opera" is plural for the Latin word *opus*, which means "a work").

At the same time, solo singing developed rapidly as a new art form. Musicians called this new style of singing, which followed the natural flow of the words, monody (see page 20). A group of musicians and literary people called the Florentine *Camerata*—based in Florence, Italy—was determined to develop this new art form. They believed that the words in an opera were more important than the music and that

THE DOCTRINE OF THE AFFECTIONS

Baroque composers felt it was important, especially in vocal music, to indicate to a listener the particular emotions ("affections")—such as joy, anger, sadness, hate, or love —that they were trying to express. To achieve this, they used a series of musical ideas that are now called "the doctrine of the affections."

For example, in George Frideric Handel's "Hallelujah" **chorus** from the *Messiah*, the words "King of Kings and Lord of Lords" are sung on the same note to reinforce the oneness of God. In the chorus "All we like sheep have gone astray" the word "astray" is written for sopranos and tenors, with each separate melody curving and winding away from the other or "going astray." Melodies, **rhythms**, accents (directions to the performer to emphasize a particular note or notes), repeated notes, and other musical ideas

were used to strengthen the "affections" in the words. An ascending melody, in which the notes went up in **pitch** as the melody continued, was thought to express hope and enthusiasm, while a descending melody that went down in pitch represented sadness or suffering.

Below: Part of Handel's original manuscript of *Messiah*. Notice how the words "King of Kings and Lord of Lords" are all on one note—to emphasize the oneness of God.

RECITATIVE AND ARIA IN BAROQUE OPERA

Recitative and aria together form the two basic vocal elements that are characteristic of Baroque opera.

Recitative is basically sung speech. It originated in Florence in early preoperatic works and later entered opera and other styles of vocal music. The singer was usually accompanied by a keyboard instrument and perhaps a low stringed instrument, both together called the continuo. Through recitative sections the composer could give the audience important information about the development of the story. As sung speech, recitative was easily understood by the audience.

Aria is a solo song. It was usually written in a decorative fashion (see example on page 33) to show off the singer's talents, and followed a strict musical form called da capo, meaning "from the beginning." The da capo form is as follows: A (opening music), B (contrasting music), A (opening music again). Slight changes were often made to the melody of the opening music when it was repeated in the second A section.

Below and below right: The composer Claudio Monteverdi, and the title page of his opera *Orfeo*, published in Venice, Italy, in 1609.

the role of the music was to echo the meaning of the words.

The first real opera, *Euridice*, was composed by two singer-composers—Jacopo Peri (1561–1633) and Giulio Caccini (*c.*1545–1618)—in 1600 and was first performed in Florence in the same year.

Bringing opera into the Baroque era

Claudio Monteverdi's music (1567–1643) spanned both the Renaissance and Baroque eras, and he was extremely important in the development of Italian opera from the end of the 16th century and into the 17th century. He wrote at least 12 operas, only three of which survive today, including *Orfeo* (1607) and *The Coronation of*

Poppea (1642). The opera *Orfeo* tells the story of Orpheus and Euridice, and shows the influence of Peri and Caccini's earlier opera *Euridice*. It is a mixture of solo **airs** (songs) and **duets** (works sung by two singers), with **choruses**, instrumental sections, and dancing. The orchestra that Monteverdi used was extremely large for its day and included about 40 instruments. The **instrumentation** was chosen to express the particular atmosphere of each scene. For instance, the loud, rich sound of trombones was used for the scenes in hell, while soft recorders and string sounds were used for the quiet, romantic scenes.

Despite these landmark works, opera took a long time to develop in Venice, and it was not until 1637 that the first opera house opened there. However, within a short time Venice became the operatic capital of Italy.

Beginnings of French opera

An attempt was made to bring opera to Paris with the performance of several Italian works, one of which—

Egisto by Francesco Cavalli (1602–1676), the most important Italian opera composer after Monteverdi—was performed in 1646. But this opera, and even the opera Cavalli wrote for Louis XIV's marriage in 1662, was not popular in France.

French opera grew out of the *Ballet de cour* ("court ballet")—entertainments made up of ballet, music, and drama written by several composers and dramatists. They were most popular in the early 17th century, when they were performed for the French royal court. But the move toward a true French operatic style began with the composer Jean-Baptiste Lully (1632–1687).

Lully's operas began with a piece of instrumental music called an **overture**. The first part of the overture was slow and majestic, and the second part fast. His orchestra was made up of a large section of stringed instruments, mostly violins, which gave the music a bright, crisp sound. He also used flutes and oboes, and—especially for battle scenes—trumpets and drums. The

Below: A painting of a performance of Lully's opera *Armide* at the Opera House in Paris in 1686.

recitatives carefully fitted the words, so that the audience could also appreciate the poetry. Lively choruses contrasted with the slower recitative sections. Finally, Lully pleased his audiences by including elegant ballet—always a favorite with the French.

Lully's first real opera was *Cadmus and Hermione*, performed in 1673. With the success of this and further operas Lully became the main composer of French opera at this time.

Beginnings of English opera

English opera owed much to Lully's theatrical works. From his operas came the French overture (as it came to be called), which began the music. Also influential was Lully's use of the orchestra to portray exciting scenes on stage, such as battles and storms. Finally, ballet appeared in English opera as a direct French influence.

English opera grew out of the masque—a court entertainment set on a stage with background scenery, which included music and dancing by costumed performers. The first English opera, *The Siege of Rhodes*, was written by several composers and was performed in 1659. It included both recitative and chorus in a single connected story. Sadly, the musical manuscript did not survive.

The first English opera that has survived is *Orpheus and Euridice* by Matthew Locke (c.1622–1677), who also contributed to *The Siege of Rhodes*. Although Locke called *Orpheus* a masque, it contained only music

and song, and was written in the style of early Italian opera.

However, it was Henry Purcell (1659–1695) who was the most gifted early English composer of opera. Purcell had written many types of music fashionable at the time, but began to compose for the theater during the last 10 years of his life. He wrote only one true opera, *Dido and Aeneas* (1689), but it includes his most famous vocal **piece** (musical composition): "When I Am Laid in Earth," known as *Dido's Lament*. In this music Purcell cleverly repeats the same bass melody over and over again (this is called a ground bass) below the melody sung by Queen Dido. This technique created a strong emotional atmosphere in which the drama of the piece unfolded.

Purcell also wrote music for more than 40 stage plays and

he composed five semioperas—made up of music, song, and some spoken dialogue—including *King Arthur* (1691) and *The Fairy Queen* (1692). After Purcell's death English opera practically disappeared. Instead the English developed a taste for Italian opera and its composers.

Beginnings of German opera

Italian opera also dominated the scene in Germany during the first half of the 17th century. Since Germany was so close to Italy—on the other side of the Alps—it relied mainly on Italy to supply it with operas.

For the first 75 years of the 17th century very few German operas were written. However, because northern Germany was farther from Italy, a few northern German composers began to compose operas, even though the Lutheran church of the time considered stage performances to be sinful. Many German operas written at this time were called **singspiel**—an opera with spoken dialogue.

The first opera house in Europe outside Italy was built in Hamburg in 1678. Its opening was celebrated with a performance of *Adam and Eve* by Johann Theile (1646–1724). Many of Germany's opera composers were based around Hamburg at this time,

Right: Handel's father is said to have disapproved of his son's interest in music and refused to allow him an instrument. But a clavichord was smuggled into the attic so that Handel could learn to play it.

such as Reinhard Keiser (1674–1739), who became a central figure in German Baroque opera. He was also a major influence on George Frideric Handel (1685–1759), who used music from a number of Keiser's works in his own compositions.

Master of Baroque opera and vocal music

George Frideric Handel was one of the greatest composers of the Baroque age. He excelled in both vocal and instrumental music, although his natural leaning was toward opera. Handel lived most of his life in England, where he moved in the highest circles of nobility.

The Baroque era was a time when musicians and composers would travel throughout Europe to study and perform music. This made the music of composers such as Handel very international. Throughout his life Handel's music was influenced by the European countries he had visited, but mostly by Italy. As a young composer he spent over three years there, meeting Italian composers like Arcangelo Corelli (1653–1713). In Italy he also came into contact with opera, as well as all of the instrumental music forms of the day.

In England an important part of Handel's work was to write music for royal and national celebrations such as

coronations. For these occasions he wrote in a brilliant orchestral style that was often highlighted by the use of trumpets and drums.

Below: Handel as a confident young composer in his 20s.

Musical gifts

Handel was born in Halle, Germany. It was clear from an early age that he was musically gifted, and Handel's father eventually allowed him to be taught the harpsichord (see page 51), violin, and organ, as well as music theory and composition.

In 1702 he was offered an organist's position in Halle. The job was for one year only, after which he finally left his hometown of Halle and moved to Hamburg—the cultural center of northern Germany.

The first operas

In Hamburg Handel was offered a job at the opera house first as a violinist and later as a harpsichordist. It was here that he really began to compose operas, starting with *Almira* in 1705, which met with much success. In 1706 he left for Florence specifically to study opera. His opera *Rodrigo* was performed there the following year. He then wrote two more operas that were successful: *Acis and Galatea*, which was performed in Naples in 1708, and *Agrippina*, performed in Venice a year later. Both were praised for the high quality of the music and for their dramatic content, a rare mix in operas of the time.

On returning to Germany he was appointed *Kapellmeister* (musician in charge of church music) to the Elector of Hanover, the future King George I of England. In 1710 he visited London, where his opera *Rinaldo* was performed a year later to such acclaim that he decided to make London his permanent home. When Handel arrived in London, he found it obsessed with Italian opera, so he immediately set about writing operas in the Italian style. His many successes with performances of *Rinaldo* and with *Giulio Cesare* ("Julius Caesar") in 1724 brought him fame and financial security for another 20 years.

Handel's oratorios
Handel wanted to expand on the stories from classical mythology that opera composers used in their librettos—the words or text in

Above: A painting of the famous castrato Carlo Broschi (1705–1782), known to his public as Farinelli.

THE SUPREMACY OF THE SINGER

As the fashionable Italian opera began to spread across Europe, virtuoso singers—performers with great technical ability—were suddenly in great demand to sing the more challenging vocal lines of this new art form. Female singers were also needed and began to enter the previously male-only profession of public singing for the first time.

The castrato—a male singer who has had a special operation before the age of 10 to preserve the top range of his voice—suddenly assumed an important role in nonreligious music. The castrato voice had already been used in church music to supply a strong, high male voice and now became an essential requirement for opera. Between the years 1650 to 1750 castratos reached the height of their popularity.

The finest singers—male and female—came from Italy, where voice training had reached a high level of technique and creativity. This new operatic singing style later came to be known as bel canto ("beautiful singing").

Audiences flocked to hear the vocal acrobatics of the famous singers of the day, often more than to enjoy the composer's music. Convinced of their ability to draw crowds, the singers became extremely self-important and began to demand huge fees. They often insisted on their parts being rewritten or new solos being composed for them to show off their vocal skills. Such demands often caused loud public disputes between the opera promoter, composer, and singer.

operas—by using stories from the Bible. However, the Bishop of London refused to allow operatic librettos of a religious nature. So Handel turned back to the oratorio. The oratorio was an opera without acting, costumes, or scenery; therefore the cost of performing an oratorio was far less than that of performing an opera. Also, expensive virtuoso singers were not needed in oratorio, since the parts were not as difficult to sing, and acting ability was unimportant. Handel had written oratorios before, during the time he spent in Italy.

Musical variety

With the performance of *Esther* in 1732 Handel began a new series of oratorios. In these works he drew on his experience as an opera composer. But now, since staging was not required (the performers simply stood to sing their parts), he could direct his efforts solely to the music.

The oratorio is like an opera, only without acting, costumes, or scenery

---

Handel's oratorios are never boring or tedious to listen to. He alternated the slower recitative sections with beautiful arias and then added boisterous choruses and instrumental sections. It was this musical variety that brought him great success with

Above: Handel (on the right) conducts one of his oratorios.

such works as *Israel in Egypt* (1739), *Messiah* (1742), *Judas Maccabaeus* (1747), and *Solomon* (1749).

Court activities

Handel's first court works were for Queen Anne. She asked him to write a religious composition for the signing of the Peace of Utrecht in 1713, for which he wrote the "Utrecht" *Te Deum*. He pleased her again by writing an ode for her birthday, perhaps causing her to grant him a yearly payment of £200. In 1714 Queen Anne died, and Handel's old employer George of Hanover became king of England.

The *Water Music* and the *Royal Fireworks Music* are Handel's best-known court pieces. Both are **suites**—works in several short **movements** (independent sections within a work), usually in the same **key**, that are made up mostly of dance forms. The *Water Music* was written for a royal water pageant in 1717. The king and court left the palace at Whitehall in London and sailed down the Thames River to Chelsea. The musicians followed on a big barge. At Chelsea they ate a magnificent feast. The royal party then returned to Westminster, with the musicians again trailing behind.

On the signing of the Peace of Aix-la-Chapelle, which marked the end of the War of the Austrian Succession (1740–1748), a grand fireworks display was planned. Handel was asked to write music for this spectacular event. He wrote the *Royal Fireworks Music* for a huge orchestra so that it could be heard above the fireworks. The event, however, ended in disaster when the entire building that housed the fireworks caught fire.

Composer in residence

Handel wrote church music for most of his life according to the needs of a particular job or patron. For example, in 1717 Handel was appointed composer-in-residence to the Earl of Carnarvon at Cannons, the earl's home 10 miles north of London. Here the Duke of Chandos (as the earl became in 1719) had a private chapel. Handel wrote some of his best church music to be performed there, including 11 works now known as the Chandos **anthems**. The anthems were Handel's first attempt at grand religious music, and there are strong emotional contrasts in the music, from moments of thrilling passion to moments of quiet thoughtfulness.

After the Chandos anthems Handel wrote most of his church music for the Chapel Royal (the king's chapel in London), where he became resident composer in 1723.

Instrumental music

Handel and other composers of opera and vocal music wrote instrumental music as well, and the Baroque era saw a new and growing interest in this type of music. More such works of excellent quality were being written, and instrumental music was slowly becoming as popular as vocal music.

The use of specific instrumentation began in the Baroque era. This new approach was a big turnaround from the Renaissance era, when composers wrote for unspecified instruments. At that time the instrumentation for a performance would be decided by the composer depending on the musicians and instruments that were available. This practice, however, also continued throughout the Baroque era.

Early Baroque composers used a wide collection of wind instruments— such as the brilliant-sounding cornett— some of which disappeared over the following centuries. Stringed instruments were represented by both the viol and violin families.

Viols and violins

Viols came in several sizes and were played vertically, resting on the lap. They had frets— strips of gut, bone, ivory, or wood that were fixed to the fingerboard, which is the part of the instrument where the player's fingers press down on the strings to sound the different notes, much like the modern guitar. Viols were played with a bow—a wooden stick with strands of horsehair attached to it that is pulled across the strings to make a sound. The greatest viol player of his time was probably the French composer Marin Marais (1656–1728), who wrote over 500 works for viols. His compositions were greatly admired for their musical variety and emotional expression.

The various instruments in the violin family were also made in several sizes—violin, viola (a larger and deeper-sounding version of the violin), cello, and double bass. Like viols, instruments in the violin family are also played with a bow, but they have no frets. The violin and viola are played with one end under the chin, and the cello and double bass rest on the floor. By the end of the 17th century the viol family had been

Above: The French composer Marin Marais plays a viol in this Baroque portrait.

Right: This 18th-century painting shows what Venice looked like in Vivaldi's day as seen from the Grand Canal, with the Doge's Palace (right), St. Mark's Square (center), and the campanile (left).

replaced almost completely by the violin family, encouraged by the beautiful new violins being made by Antonio Stradivari (c.1644–1737).

One of the greatest composers for the violin was the Italian composer Antonio Vivaldi.

The instrumental concerto

Antonio Vivaldi (1678–1741) is one of the most important composers of the Baroque period. He wrote much vocal and church music, and a number of operas and sonatas. In the Baroque era the sonata was a work for one or several instruments, often accompanied by a keyboard, which was written in more than one movement (a self-contained section within a larger work). Later, in the Classical era the sonata also came to mean a single movement of a composition written in a specific musical form (see box on page 53).

However, Vivaldi is most famous for his development of the **concerto**. Early in the Baroque era the concerto was a work for voices and a group of instruments that was called the concerto grosso. Yet Vivaldi's concertos were among the first to

Above: A portrait of Vivaldi and a violin, for which he wrote many great works.

realize the solo possibilities of a wide variety of instruments playing on their own and prepared the way for the one-instrument concerto of the Classical era. Vivaldi was also one of the first composers to use an important new instrument—the clarinet.

The pull of music

Vivaldi's first instrument was the violin. It was given to him by his father Giovanni—a violinist in the orchestra of St. Mark's Cathedral in Venice. Despite instructing him in the violin, Giovanni wanted his son to enter the priesthood. Vivaldi went along with his father's wishes and took orders in 1703, but the pull of music was too great for him. He left after a year to take a job as *maestro di violino* ("violin master") at a girls' music academy in Venice, where he remained for most of his life.

THE RISE OF THE PUBLIC CONCERT

The idea of performing concerts for those other than the nobility to enjoy was new to the Baroque era. Music had always taken a major role at grand occasions, but the general public was not usually allowed to be present at these events. In the royal courts concerts were also common—the reputation of the court was improved by the splendor and frequency of its private musical entertainments. But again, most of these concerts were confined to members of the nobility.

During the Baroque era, however, concerts began to be set up for the general public as well. In France and Italy during the 16th and 17th centuries the first public concerts were held in education establishments. In Germany at this time such entertainments were usually set up by a *Collegium Musicum* (music society or guild).

Yet although these concerts were public, it was not always easy to obtain admission. In England concerts were often on a "subscription" basis—the concert-goer paid for several concerts in advance. They also paid at the door as people often do today. But in either case admission was not cheap. In Germany, France, and Italy, although concerts promoted by educational establishments and societies were free, they were only open to their own members and invited guests, and because of this, remained middle-class entertainments only available to the "well-bred."

However, it was London that led Europe as a concert city. As early as 1672 a series of concerts was organized in London by the violinist John Banister (1630–1679). In 1678 a further series of concerts was set up Thomas Britton (1644–1714) in Clerkenwell, London. Although Britton was only a humble coal-seller, he was also a self-taught musician

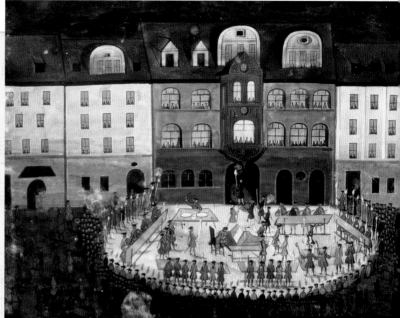

Above: A watercolor of a festive music concert at the *Collegium Musicum* in Jena, Germany, in about 1740.

and scholar, and knew many of London's most cultured people, including members of the nobility. Once the trend had been started, concerts continued to increase in popularity, and by the beginning of the 18th century London could boast several concert establishments.

These first public concerts were not held in a concert hall as it is known today, but anywhere where there was enough space. This could be a room in someone's home or, in the summer, outside. In London outdoor concerts were often held in the Vauxhall Gardens, which opened in 1736. A large space was important for the concert. More people could attend, which would earn more for the concert promoter. London's first recorded public concert was held in a tavern, the Mitre Inn, in 1664.

The demand for concerts eventually spread outside the city—in 1748 the first public concert hall in Europe built specifically for that purpose opened in Oxford, England.

Vivaldi's concertos

Vivaldi wrote over 500 concertos, including over 200 for violin and others for bassoon, cello, oboe, flute, recorder, and even mandolin. Most of them (about two-thirds) are for solo instrument and orchestra. Vivaldi gave the solo instruments more importance by writing more interesting and exciting parts for them to play. He included a number of different violin techniques in his violin concertos. For instance, he occasionally used a mute—a peglike device that is fitted over the bridge of a stringed instrument to soften the sound—and also pizzicato (plucking the strings).

Most of Vivaldi's concertos are written in three movements in a quick-slow-quick pattern. He was the first composer to regularly use ritornello form for his quick movements. During the ritornello (repeat) sections the solo instrument remains silent, and the orchestra (called the ripieno) plays. The alternations between solo instrument, or instruments, and the orchestra add great variety to the music.

Invention of the program

Vivaldi's most famous concertos are a set of four for violin known as *The Four Seasons.* They are based on the themes of spring, summer, fall, and winter, and are part of a series of 12 entitled "The Contest between Harmony and Invention." Each has a program attached to it—a sonnet, or poem, describing the thoughts and feelings suggested to the composer by each season. Vivaldi was one of the first to attach programs to his instrumental works—a practice that became popular by the 19th century.

Vivaldi's influence

Vivaldi's skill as a composer was so admired during his lifetime that he even influenced several of his older contemporaries, who changed their composing style in the middle of their careers. The Italian composers Giuseppe Tartini (1692–1770) and Pietro Antonio Locatelli (1695–1764) were influenced by his contrasting of the solo and tutti (when all the instruments play together) sections of the concerto. Similarly, J.S. Bach was so impressed by Vivaldi's concertos that he made **arrangements** of several of them for other instruments as a study exercise. The most famous of

Above: A portrait of the Italian composer Domenico Scarlatti "the father of modern keyboard technique."

Below: This painting shows the Louvre (right) in Paris, France, c.1666, around the time the composer François Couperin was born.

these arrangements is a concerto for four harpsichords, which Bach arranged from a concerto for four violins.

Keyboard music in Italy and France

Although Vivaldi wrote a large number of musical compositions, he did not write much music for the keyboard, despite the fact that this instrument was extremely popular at the time. In Italy the master of keyboard compositions was a slightly younger contemporary of Vivaldi's—Domenico Scarlatti (1685–1757). Scarlatti was one of three great composers of keyboard music in Italy and France who bridged the Baroque and Classical eras. The other two were the Frenchmen François Couperin and Jean-Philippe Rameau.

Scarlatti is considered to be "the father of modern keyboard technique." He was born the same year as Bach and Handel, and was the son of the composer Alessandro Scarlatti (1660–1725). Although Domenico composed operas,

Above: An 18th-century painting of the French composer Jean-Philippe Rameau holding a violin of the period.

concertos, and church music, his reputation rests on the 555 keyboard sonatas written toward the end of his life. The sonatas, which he called *essercizi* ("exercises"), were in one movement. They varied from simple teaching pieces for his pupils, to much more difficult music suited to more professional players. Scarlatti was an extremely skillful keyboard composer. He used crossed hands (the right hand crossing over the left or the left over the right to play notes at the other end of the keyboard), quickly repeated notes, and wide leaps for both hands, from one area of the keyboard to the next—all unusual techniques for the period. In his sonatas Scarlatti used many harmonies and chords that were new and unusual in his day.

Elegance and harmony

François Couperin (1668–1733) was known as "Couperin le Grand" to distinguish him from a large family of lesser-skilled musicians of the same name. His 225 harpsichord works were grouped in *ordres* (suites). Many of the pieces had fanciful titles—descriptions of moods, natural objects, or even portraits of people—while other movements were in traditional French dance forms, such as the **minuet**, **allemande**, **courante**, and **sarabande**. Couperin decorates the melodies of these pieces by adding

many musical embellishments and ornaments—extra notes squeezed in between the main notes of the tune to make the music sound more graceful and elegant (see page 33).

Born 15 years after Couperin, Jean-Philippe Rameau (1683–1764) published his first harpsichord pieces in 1706. They showed the influence of Couperin in their descriptive titles, such as *Les soupirs* ("The sighs") and *La poule* ("The hen"), and in their use of French dances. During the early part of Rameau's life he was known as a theorist, and in 1722 he wrote a book on modern harmony. The theory of harmony was a strong interest of his, so it is not surprising that he used inventive harmony in his works, such as when the music moves quickly from one key to another.

As well as their keyboard pieces, Scarlatti, Couperin, and Rameau also wrote vocal music. Rameau in

particular was a successful opera composer; his *Castor and Pollux* (1737) was enormously popular in Paris when it was first performed.

Baroque cantatas

One of the most important categories of vocal music composed during the Baroque era was the **cantata**—a vocal work written in several movements for soloists and chorus, accompanied by an orchestra.

The first cantatas were similar to opera: they were written for one or two voices, with accompaniment, and contained both recitative and aria (see page 34). Yet unlike opera, cantatas were performed only in concert halls, not in the theater.

The cantata's early development was centered around Rome, where the nobility were keen patrons of music, and there was a tradition of vocal music and good singing. In Germany composers such as Michael Praetorius

(1571–1621) composed vocal church music for different combinations of voices and instruments based on well-known **hymn** tunes called **chorales**. The church cantata developed from these works and always ended with a simple arrangement of the hymn melody in which the congregation would join the **choir**.

The greatest composer of the church cantata was Johann Sebastian Bach, who wrote over 300 such works, 200 of which survive today.

The Bach dynasty

The Bach family of musicians goes back to the mid-16th century and forward to the early 19th century. More than 53 family members can be traced as musicians, organists, and even instrument manufacturers working in central Germany, where musical traditions were strong.

The first known musical Bach—Johannes Hans Bach—was Johann

THE STORY OF MUSIC

Sebastian's great grandfather. All types of musicianship were drilled into the male members of the Bach family, usually by the father or another close male family member. Not all of the Bach family were composers, but those who were organists may also have composed as part of their church duties. Maria Barbara's father, the organist Johann Michael Bach (1648–1694), wrote vocal church music and organ music. Johann Bernhard (1676–1749), also an organist, wrote orchestral music that was admired and studied by Johann Sebastian. The last surviving member of the family, Wilhelm Friedrich Ernst (1749–1845), a grandson of Johann Sebastian, was a teacher and a keyboard player as well as a composer.

A humble genius

Johann Sebastian Bach (1685–1750) spent his whole life in northern Germany. Although he gained recognition as a keyboard player at the time, especially as an organist, there were a few other composers far better known in Europe than he was. Yet there are many today who consider him to be the greatest composer of all time.

Johann Sebastian thought of himself as a competent musician and composer, working to the best of his ability for his various patrons, but ultimately to the glory of

Above: J.S. Bach, considered by many today to be the greatest composer of all time.

Below: J.S. Bach's father—Johann Ambrosius Bach.

God. Many of his musical manuscripts are inscribed, in various ways "to the Glory of God." Even the small book of works collected for his son Wilhelm Friedemann is inscribed I. N. J. (*in nomine Jesu*, meaning "in the name of Jesus"), while his religious vocal works are regularly inscribed J. J. (*Jesu, juva*, meaning "Jesus, help"). Johann Sebastian composed in every type of music around at the time except opera.

Early years

Johann Sebastian's first tutor was his father, Johann Ambrosius; and when he died in 1795, the young Johann was taken in by his organist brother Johann Christoph, who gave him his first music lessons. At the age of 15 Johann Sebastian was sent as a choirboy to Lüneberg, where he completed his education.

Johann Sebastian took his first professional job in 1703 as a violinist in the court orchestra at Weimar. But a more tempting organist's job came his way the same year at Arnstadt, where he remained for four years. After a series of organist jobs he returned to Weimar to take up the position of court organist and chamber music musician for the Duke of Saxe-Weimar—a post he was to hold for 10 years.

Organ music at Weimar

Johann Sebastian wrote organ music throughout his life, but it was at Weimar

Right: This watercolor shows Weimar, Germany, around the time J.S. Bach lived there. It is where he wrote many of his most famous organ compositions.

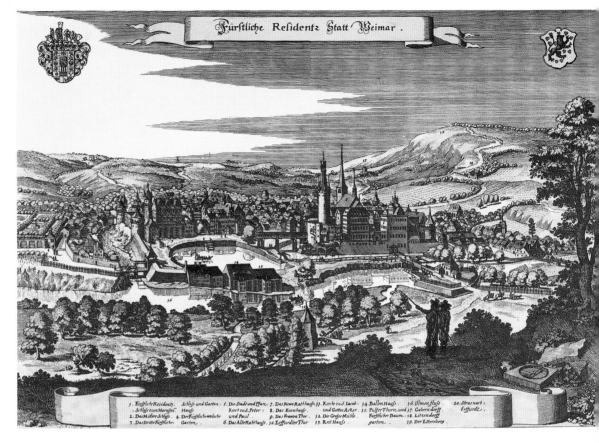

that he wrote the most. During these years he also made a name for himself as one of the finest organists of his day. The duke liked his playing and encouraged him to compose for the church services.

Bach's early organ works show the influence of other composers, such as Georg Böhm (1661–1733) and Dietrich Buxtehude (c.1637–1707), who was regarded as the greatest organist in northern Germany.

During his time at Weimar Johann Sebastian wrote most of the *Orgelbüchlein* ("Little organ book")— a collection of short chorale preludes. The chorale prelude was a solo work for organ based on a chorale. Johann Sebastian wrote this collection as a work for teaching music students.

Johann Sebastian also wrote many **preludes** and **fugues**. These works generally began with a lively prelude (introductory music), followed by a fugue—a movement written for two

or more parts in which the opening melody is taken up by every part in turn. Several of Bach's organ works have become well known to modern audiences through later orchestral arrangements, especially those by the **conductor** Leopold Stokowski (1882–1977). They include the famous Toccata and Fugue in D and the Passacaglia and Fugue in C minor.

Orchestral and chamber music

In 1717 Johann Sebastian took the post of music director to Prince Leopold of Anhalt-Cöthen, who employed a small orchestra and was especially fond of **secular** instrumental music. For the first time in his career Johann Sebastian had no church duties, so he threw himself into composing instrumental music.

Dating from this period are the Brandenburg Concertos. This set of six works, each with a different instrumentation, was commissioned by Christian Ludwig, the Margrave of Brandenburg. In a striking display of modesty, on presenting the works Johann Sebastian asked the Margrave not to judge "their imperfections too harshly." The Brandenburg Concertos date from 1721 and are celebrated for their imaginative **orchestration** and technical musical virtuosity. In them Johann Sebastian abandoned the concerto grosso and used unusual combinations of different solo instruments. They also marked the beginning of the harpsichord concerto as a new form.

While at Cöthen, he began composing a series of orchestral suites made up of an important opening movement, or **overture**, followed by several dance movements. In Johann Sebastian's day an entire suite was also sometimes called an overture because it was the longest part of the piece. The third suite includes a movement entitled "Air" that since Bach's time has been arranged for many different instruments. It is sometimes known as

---

J.S. Bach wrote keyboard music in every style known in the Baroque period

---

"Air on the G string" from the violin arrangement by the violinist August Wilhelmj (1845–1908).

Johann Sebastian also wrote chamber music at Cöthen. It is thought that much of this has been lost, but some important works have survived. There are the three sonatas and three partitas (partita is another name for suite) for solo violin, and the six suites for solo cello. The cello pieces are the first works ever written for solo cello. The second violin partita includes a movement called

"Chaconne," which—like the Air mentioned previously—has since been arranged for many other instruments. The Spanish guitarist Andrés Segovia (1893–1987) did a very famous arrangement of it for the guitar.

Johann Sebastian's solo violin and cello works are often played today. They are more advanced than most of the works for stringed instruments written by composers who came before him, both in their use of harmony and in their understanding of the particular performing techniques of stringed instruments.

Keyboard music

Johann Sebastian wrote keyboard music in every style known during the Baroque period. He wrote several sets of suites and partitas, variations, and many other keyboard works. Most of them were composed after he left Cöthen.

In his music for keyboard Johann Sebastian was greatly influenced by French and Italian composers, as well as by German. He calls his Partita in B minor "Overture in the French style" because the first movement begins slowly and majestically, while the second half is **rhythmic** and lively—just like the overtures of the French composer Lully. French dances also feature in many of Bach's

Below: The first page of the First Prelude from the manuscript of J.S. Bach's *Well-tempered Clavichord.* It was a collection of 12 preludes and 12 fugues, each written in a different key, which was published in 1722.

keyboard works. The influence of Italy can be heard in a concerto written in 1735, which Bach called "Concerto in the Italian style." Here the harpsichord's two keyboards (each keyboard has a different sound) imitate the parts of the solo concerto instrument and orchestra in the style of concertos written by Italian composers such as Corelli.

Around 1742 Bach wrote a piece called "Air with Thirty Different Variations." It was commissioned by the Russian ambassador in Dresden for his harpsichordist Johann Gottlieb Goldberg (1727–1756) and is now known as the Goldberg Variations. This work is famous for its enormous range of styles and emotions—all of which are connected by an underlying theme—and is one of the greatest works in variation form.

A final move

In 1720 Prince Leopold married. His wife was not musical, and it is thought this may have caused Johann Sebastian to look for a new job. A chance came in 1723 when he was offered the position of *Kantor* (musical director) of St. Thomas's church in Leipzig—a position he was to keep for the rest of his life.

The Leipzig churches required 58 cantatas each year, as well as music for special political and religious occasions. Johann Sebastian would compose a new cantata every month whenever possible, but he also reworked and reused earlier pieces. Today, about 200 of his cantatas have survived, although he is thought to have written many more. He also wrote **motets** and other church music, including the monumental *St. John Passion* (1724) and *St. Matthew Passion* (1727). Passions are musical works that express the suffering and death of Christ. In these passions the

Above: A portrait of J.S. Bach is set in the middle of a stained-glass window in the St. Thomas Church in Leipzig, where he was a choirmaster for almost 30 years.

chorus takes on the role of the crowd at Christ's crucifixion, and the voices of Pontius Pilates and Jesus are sung by soloists. The text for both passions comes directly from the Bible.

Music compositions were not the only things Johann Sebastian left behind. He fathered 20 children, although 13 of them died in infancy. However, four of his sons became well-known composers—William Friedemann, Johann Christoph Friedrich, Johann Christian, and Carl Philipp Emanuel. Carl Philipp Emanuel was to become the most famous Bach of the Classical era.

CHAPTER 4

The Classical Era

The term "Classical music" refers to music that is thought to be serious and lasting. The period from about 1750 to 1820 is usually called the Classical era.

When people use the term "Classical music," they are usually referring to music that they consider to be serious and lasting, as opposed to light-hearted, up-to-date but short-lived "popular music." In the history of music, however, the term "classical" is used in a more specific way. The period from about 1750 to 1820 is usually called the Classical era. In this sense the word "classical" refers to music that is thought to be of the highest class, or quality. Experts consider classical works to have lasting value and to form models that are worth studying in later periods, and the term is used

in a similar way in architecture, literature, and other art forms. Such classical works have been created throughout the history of music, but so many were produced during the second half of the 18th century and the beginning of the 19th that this period is now referred to as classical.

Earlier musical works had been written to accompany dance, drama, and religious ceremonies, but most of the music of the Classical era was written and enjoyed for its own sake. Composers dedicated themselves to writing music that could be appreciated by itself. The classical era produced three of the world's greatest

Above: Ancient Greek architecture, like the Temple of Athena Nike in the Acropolis in Athens, is called "classical" because it is said to embody perfect proportions and so be a template for beauty and style. Such classical architecture has continued to inspire and influence architects over the centuries.

composers ever—Haydn, Mozart, and Beethoven. Their works created a new audience for music—people who wanted to attend concerts and listen to music played by soloists and orchestras. This new approach to music began with a composer who today is considered to be much less important than the other three "greats," but who had a strong influence on them all—C.P.E. Bach.

The famous son

Carl Philipp Emanuel Bach (1714–1788) was born in Weimar, Germany, the second oldest son of Johann Sebastian Bach, who gave him his first music lessons. Emanuel went on to study law and philosophy at Frankfurt University, but after graduating, he turned again to music and moved to Berlin. He soon became a highly respected composer and keyboard player. As a young man, he was naturally influenced by his father's music, but later he developed his own style that had more in common with other young composers of his day.

When Emanuel was 24, his talents were noticed by Crown Prince

Above: C.P.E. Bach, Johann Sebastian's most famous son.

Frederick of Prussia, who hired him as his royal harpsichordist. Frederick was himself a composer and a skilled flute player. One of Emanuel's main duties was to accompany the prince's flute solos on the harpsichord—a keyboard instrument similar to the piano, but with strings that are plucked by a quill rather than hit with a hammer. Only two years after Emanuel took the post, his employer became King Frederick II of Prussia (later known as "Frederick the Great"). Emanuel remained in the king's employment for almost 30 years. In 1767, however, he was offered the post of *Kantor*—the person responsible for music and **choir** training—for five of the most

Left: King Frederick II of Prussia performs on the flute, while C.P.E. Bach (seated on his left) accompanies him on the harpsichord.

important churches in Hamburg. Emanuel accepted the job and remained in Hamburg until his death in 1788.

THE SYMPHONY

The word symphony comes from a Greek word that means "sounding together." As a musical form it has meant various things at different times throughout history. In the Renaissance and Baroque periods it could mean a composition either for an orchestra or for voices and an orchestra. It could also mean an **overture**—an instrumental work that is played to introduce a ballet, play, or opera—or an interlude, which is an instrumental work played in the middle of a larger work or between the acts of a play or an opera.

By the time C.P.E. Bach was writing his first symphonies, the word had come to mean a composition for orchestra, usually in three **movements**, or **parts**. In his symphonies the first movement was usually fast, the second was slow and sad, and the third was fast and cheerful. Then, from about 1765 the symphony became an instrumental work in four movements. The first and fourth movements were quicker than the slow second movement, and the third movement used a dance form such as the **minuet** combined with a **trio**. The trio, so called because it was played by three musicians, formed the middle section of the minuet. This structure of the symphony remained the same until the early 19th century, when Ludwig von Beethoven developed the symphony further by adding more instruments to the orchestra to expand its range of sounds.

Above: Detail from an 18th-century painting of the symphony orchestra at the court of Vienna.

The musical rebel

Emanuel's early work was influenced by his father's **polyphonic** music, which was mainly made up of many strands of **melody** woven together, as in a **fugue**. However, as time went on, Emanuel turned against this kind of composition because he felt it was trying to be over complicated just for

---

From 1765 the symphony became an instrumental work in four movements

---

the sake of it. Instead, Emanuel's music moved toward a new homophonic style, which meant that it was made up of a single melody played by one instrument, with other, less important instruments supporting this melody. The main melody was often played on an instrument with a high range, such as the violin or flute. During the Classical era composers began writing their compositions more in this way, although the old polyphonic style was still popular for church music.

Emanuel's symphonies

In Emanuel's day the great centers of symphony composition were the cities of Vienna in Austria and Berlin and Mannheim in Germany. Emanuel and his colleague Carl Heinrich Graun (*c.*1703–1759) were among the leading German composers in this field. Emanuel wrote about 20 lively symphonies, all of which were filled with sudden **modulations**—changes of **key**. His symphonies often called for an unusual choice of instruments, but Emanuel stuck firmly to the traditional three-movement symphony form. The movements were often played without a break in between.

Exploring the keyboard

In addition to writing symphonies, Emanuel wrote many keyboard works, using harmonies that were unusual for the time. Emanuel was known as an excellent keyboard player. His favorite instrument was the clavichord—a rectangular keyboard instrument in which the strings are struck by a hammer, not plucked mechanically as they are in a harpsichord. Toward the end of his life, however, when the clavichord fell out of fashion, he composed mostly for the piano.

Emanuel wrote his first book of keyboard works in 1742 and a second in 1744. An important new musical form began to emerge in them—the sonata form (see box on right).

Between 1753 and 1762 he wrote *Essay on the True Art of Keyboard Playing*, a book that was later used by both Mozart and Beethoven to teach their pupils. It provided musicians with a perfect guide to the playing of keyboard instruments, and it is still used by students and teachers today.

A man of influence

It was Emanuel's keyboard sonatas that had the greatest influence on other composers. His style of using unique changes of key and unusual **rhythms** was later adopted by Haydn for his own sonatas. Haydn admitted, "Whoever knows me well will see how much I owe to Carl Philipp Emanuel Bach." Mozart also had praise for Emanuel: "Those of us who can do what is right learned from him."

Above: In the 18th century Berlin was one of the great centers of symphony composition.

SONATA FORM

Originally, a sonata was simply a **piece** of music to be played rather than sung. In the 18th century it became a piece of music for one or two instruments written in two to four movements. It was also during this time that the first movement came to be composed in a special pattern called sonata form. This pattern was to become the most important musical form of the Classical era. C.P.E. Bach helped shape the sonata form, and it was later perfected by such composers as Haydn and Mozart.

The sonata form has three main parts: exposition, development, and recapitulation. The exposition "exposes," or introduces, the musical **themes** of the piece to the listener. In the development part the themes are "developed," or explored in a contrasting style to the exposition. This second part ends with a return to the main theme. The recapitulation "recapitulates," or repeats the musical themes, more or less as they were in the exposition but with slight changes.

The sonata form was so useful and popular that it was also used for other types of musical composition, such as symphonies (which are really sonatas written for a full orchestra) and quartets (sonatas written for four instruments). Sonata form was also used for movements other than the first one, and Beethoven even wrote a string quartet in which all four movements were in sonata form.

Left: Well known for his wit and good humor, Haydn was a popular figure in Viennese musical circles.

Great musical revolutionary

Joseph Haydn (1732–1809) was one of the world's greatest musical revolutionaries. He developed melody, **harmony**, and musical structure to a point they had never reached before and wrote some of the most exciting music of the Classical era.

Haydn was also known for his wit and good humor. He composed in all the different musical forms of his day: church music, oratorios, operas, symphonies, **concertos**, as well as chamber and keyboard music. Haydn's influence was particularly strong in the development of the Classical symphony and string quartet.

A voice of his own

Franz Joseph Haydn was born into a musical family in the Austrian village of Rohrau. His career started early when a relative noticed what a fine singing voice the boy had. The relative persuaded Haydn's parents to allow him to teach the child singing, violin, and the clavier. Haydn worked hard, and at eight years old he was asked to join the famous Vienna Boys'

Choir at St. Stephen's Cathedral in Vienna. He stayed with the choir until the age of 17, when his voice broke and he could no longer sing soprano.

Haydn decided to stay in Vienna and give lessons in violin, clavier, and singing. He also worked as an accompanist to Niccola Antonio Porpora (1686–1766), an Italian singing teacher and composer, who taught him the craft of composing.

Below: St. Stephen's Cathedral in Vienna, where Joseph Haydn sang in the famous Vienna Boys' Choir.

The string quartet

Before Haydn's time string quartet music had consisted of stiff, formal compositions, none of which have survived to the present day. The first examples of more mature string quartets that did survive are by Haydn, who developed and shaped this form of music to such a degree that it became hugely popular and was taken up by other composers.

During his early years as a composer Haydn wrote for the musical gatherings of various counts and other members of the Austrian nobility. Most of these compositions were written for strings. In his early music for string quartets—made up of two violins, a viola, and a cello—the melody was usually played by the violins. Sometimes both the first and second violin played the melody, with the second violin playing an **octave** below. This had a practical purpose, since many of these works were serenades—light vocal or instrumental works to be played outdoors—and the second violin

Above: An engraving of Haydn (in the red coat) shows him listening to a string quartet in a private house in Vienna.

helped strengthen the melody. Violins were useful because their sound carried farther in the open air than other stringed instruments.

In the early string quartets the viola was given the most basic part of all, doing little more than filling out the harmonies of the melody. In later quartets, however, each of the four instruments was given its own important part, although the first violin remained the traditional leader of the melody.

Four-movement form

The music for string quartets gradually developed into a four-movement form. The opening movement was the longest and usually went along at a fast **tempo**. It was followed by a gentle, slow movement. Sometimes, as in his famous *Emperor* Quartet (1797), Haydn made the second movement out of a theme and variations on that theme. The third movement was usually a **minuet** and trio, based on a 17th-century French dance, that quickened the tempo. The final movement, often written in **rondo**

CHAMBER MUSIC

The term "chamber music" originally referred to music that was written to be performed in a chamber (or room), rather than in a church. This music was played by small groups of players, originally using instruments such as the recorder, harpsichord, and viol. Chamber music was written for solo instruments (one player), **duets** (two players), trios (three players), quartets (four players), quintets (five players), sextets (six players), and so on up to eight or nine players.

In chamber music each musical part is played by only one player, and all of the parts are usually considered to be of equal importance. Haydn's string quartets come under the heading of chamber music, and indeed the largest amount of chamber music has been written for string quartets. Haydn—along with Mozart, Beethoven, and Schubert—is considered to be one of the greatest composers of chamber music.

Today the term "chamber music" is still used to describe music for small groups of instruments, but it is now performed in many different places, including concert halls.

Above: Haydn sits at the harpsichord (bottom right) at a performance in the Esterházy palace.

form, was also fast, ending the piece with a flourish. Altogether Haydn wrote 83 string quartets.

Patronage

For a northern European composer in the 18th century there was only one way to make an acceptable living, and that was to be hired by a patron. This meant having the patronage of a royal court, one of the great noble families, or the church. Haydn was lucky. After working for Count Karl von Morzin, in 1761 he was offered the post of deputy music director by Hungarian Prince Anton Esterházy— the head of one of the wealthiest families in the Austrian empire. Five years later Haydn was promoted to *Kapellmeister* (music director)—a post he held for 30 years.

His duties as *Kappellmeister* for the Esterházys were to direct the musical activities of the household—training and **conducting** players and singers— as well as composing new music in whatever form he wished. As had been the case for C.P.E. Bach before him, financial support from noble and royal patrons allowed Haydn the freedom to experiment with different musical techniques and styles. While

Right: A portrait of the impresario Johann Peter Salomon, who helped make Haydn such a success in England.

working for Prince Esterházy, Haydn wrote more than 90 symphonies, 44 string quartets, and many **cantatas**, operas, and oratorios.

Great symphonist

Haydn is sometimes called the "father of the symphony." Although many other composers before and during his time were also symphonists, it was Haydn who developed the symphony into one of the most important forms in Classical music.

Most of Haydn's symphonies were written while he was employed by Prince Esterházy. He was given his own orchestra and was entirely free to try out new ideas. "I was cut off from the world," he said, "so I was forced to become original." It was Haydn who developed the symphony into a work of four contrasting movements (see box on page 52).

In 1790 Haydn was invited to London, England, by Johann Peter Salomon (1745–1815), an impresario (director and manager of operas and ballets) who paid Haydn to write six symphonies. They were a tremendous

success, and Salomon invited Haydn to visit London again in 1794. For this second visit Haydn composed his last six symphonies, nos. 99–104. They are full of striking effects, with much syncopation (changing the emphasis of beats over a measure so that strong beats become weak and weak beats become strong), exciting modulations, sudden crescendos (increasing loudness), and dramatic contrasts of loud and soft **dynamics**.

End of an era

After Haydn returned from his second successful stay in London, he renewed his association with the Esterházy family but started to spend more and more time at his own house in Vienna.

He wrote two oratorios, *The Creation* (1798) and *The Seasons* (1801), which became very popular at the time, and composed the Austrian national **anthem**. He conducted his last concert in 1803 and spent his remaining years living quietly until his death in 1809 at the age of 77. He lived much longer than other composers of his era—over twice as long as Mozart and 20 years longer than Beethoven— which gave him time to experiment and communicate his fresh ideas in an enormous number of compositions, including 104 symphonies.

Musical genius

Many believe that the composer Wolfgang Amadeus Mozart (1756–1791) was one of the greatest musical geniuses of all time. Despite the fact that he died at the age of 35, he wrote masterpieces in almost all the musical genres of his time, including operas, concertos, symphonies, sonatas, and chamber and church music. During certain periods of his life Mozart was also one of the most famous musical performers of his time, entertaining Austrian, German, French, and English royalty from the incredible age of just six years.

Child star

One of the things that made Mozart so special was that he was a child prodigy—a young person of extreme talent. He was born in Salzburg, Austria, in 1756. His father Leopold was a violinist and composer who soon noticed his son's amazing musical ability. He taught Wolfgang clavier and violin, and by the age of five the boy was composing his own keyboard pieces. When Wolfgang was only 12 years old, he wrote his first opera, *Bastien und Bastienne*, a one-act **singspiel** that was performed in a private house in Vienna.

As early as 1762 Wolfgang and his older sister Maria—known within the family as Nannerl—played harpsichord before the Elector of Bavaria in Munich, Germany, and for Empress Maria Theresa of Austria at the Imperial Court in Vienna. The following year the family began a major tour of Europe. In Paris, France, the two children played for King Louis XV, and in London, England, for King George III. Young Mozart's own compositions were first published in Paris, and in London he wrote his first symphonies and heard them performed there.

As well as being an outstanding composer, Mozart had also become an excellent violinist and keyboard player, and showed a great talent for **improvisation**—playing music without preparation and inventing passages and melodies as it went along.

Maturing with the symphony

Mozart's earliest symphonies were influenced by Johann Christian Bach (1735–1782) and Karl Friedrich Abel (1723–1787), both of whom Mozart met in London. These early works were written for a small orchestra—consisting of oboes, horns, and strings—and usually in three contrasting, quick-slow-quick movements. His later symphonies were influenced by other composers, such as Johann Stamitz (1717–1757) and his son Carl, whose works Mozart had heard on his European tours. As he gained in experience, Mozart began to use larger orchestras and often added an extra middle movement to his symphonies. By this time the symphony was beginning to become set in its final, four-movement form.

Mozart wrote for the same groups of instruments as Haydn had—wind instruments, brass, timpani, and strings—and like Haydn, he wrote for

THE MANNHEIM SCHOOL

The Mannheim school was the name given to a group of composers who worked at the court of Mannheim, Germany, during the middle of the 18th century. Mozart, who visited Mannheim four times, was greatly influenced by the music he heard there.

The Mannheim orchestra was considered to be the finest of its time, and Mannheim's small chapel became one of the most important musical centers in Europe. Exceptional musicians were drawn to it because of the quality of its players and those who composed for it.

The school's leading lights were Franz Xavier Richter (1709–1789) and Johann and Carl Stamitz. Johann Stamitz, the musical director at Mannheim, pioneered the use of the four-movement symphony form and gave woodwind instruments a more important role. The Mannheim musicians were the first to change the dynamics of sound gradually from soft to loud, instead of switching sharply between different levels of volume.

Above: A Czech postage stamp of Johann Stamitz—violinist, composer, and conductor of the Mannheim Orchestra.

whichever individual instruments were available to him at the time. He became especially fond of the clarinet, including it in some chamber and orchestral works, as well as writing an entire concerto for it. Mozart reached his peak as a symphony composer in his last four symphonies: no. 38 (the *Prague* Symphony) and nos. 39, 40, and 41, called the *Jupiter* Symphony. The last three were written during the summer of 1788. They are considered to be his greatest symphonies and are still among the most popular.

Above: Mozart gives a recital at his home for a select group of friends. His wife Constanze is seated at his side.

Mozart's concertos

Haydn did for the string quartet and symphony what Mozart did for the piano concerto. In the concertos of Mozart the orchestra and piano play an equal role in developing the music. Many of his concertos were written to be performed by an orchestra, with himself on keyboard. Mozart's first entirely original piano concerto, known as no. 5, was performed in Salzburg in 1773, with himself as the soloist. He wrote a further 26 piano concertos, all of which followed a similar pattern.

Each piece started with the orchestra playing a theme that was then repeated or developed by the pianist, who might change or add to the melody, which was then finally taken up again by the orchestra.

Mozart also wrote five violin concertos, the *Sinfonia Concertante* for violin and viola, and several concertos for solo wind instruments such as the horn and flute. His earlier works were bright and light-hearted, whereas some of his later concertos—the last of which was performed the year he died—had a very sad sound.

Performing his piano works

Throughout his life Mozart was both a performer and a composer. Playing his own works meant that he was able to earn money, while at the same time advertising his ability as a composer. He hoped there would be members of nobility in the audience who might ask him to write compositions for them. Many of Mozart's piano works were written and then performed by him for just this purpose.

The first main influence on Mozart's keyboard style was Johann Christian Bach, who for a time was composer to the London Italian opera. Mozart heard his works when

he was in London and had a high regard for him as a composer: "I respect him with all my heart," Mozart said in a letter of 1778.

Impressive string quartets

Mozart's string quartets are among his most important pieces of chamber music because of their beautiful harmonies. His first quartet was written in a single evening when he was just 14. He was touring Italy at the time, and the music shows the influence of Italian instrumental composers, such as the composer and oboist Giuseppe Sammartini (1695–1750). Yet his greatest string quartets were written after he moved to Vienna in 1781.

In 1782 Mozart heard several of Haydn's quartets. He was very excited by the way in which Haydn had developed this musical form (see page 55), and Mozart was determined to continue with his own works "where Haydn had left off." In 1785 Haydn

attended a musical gathering in Mozart's apartment in Vienna at which three new quartets by Mozart were performed. When the older composer heard them, he was astonished and told Mozart's father: "Your son is the greatest composer I know, either personally or by name." Mozart later dedicated these and three other quartets to Haydn, and Haydn's later quartets also clearly show the influence of Mozart.

Famous operas

It was through his operas that Mozart probably achieved his greatest fame. His experiments with musical form set the stage for many opera composers who came after him. At the time of Mozart's birth opera was changing. The old-style *opera seria* (serious opera) of the Baroque period, with its elaborate rules, was rapidly going out of fashion. On his travels in Italy and France Mozart saw and heard new operas in the *opera buffa* (comic

Above: Mozart, on the right, discusses his music with Haydn, for whom he had enormous respect as a composer.

THE MAGIC FLUTE

Mozart wrote his opera *The Magic Flute* in 1791, the year in which he died. He conducted the first performance himself, and the opera proved to be a great success. It was performed in Vienna an amazing 233 times over the next 10 years.

The story, about the triumph of good over evil, is a mixture of fairy tale and pantomime, and is set in ancient Egypt. The words were written in German by Emanuel Schikaneder (1770–1845), who, like Mozart, was a Freemason—a member of a secret organization pledged to brotherly love, faith, and charity. Many references to Freemasonry appear in the opera. The overture begins with three **chords**, and the opera begins and ends in three flats (when **notes** are lowered by a half step or **semitone**); it is thought that this is because the number three was important in the rituals of Freemasons. The opera was written in the style of a singspiel (a play with singing and spoken dialogue that means "sung play" in German), with a mixture of speech and song.

In *The Magic Flute* and his other operas Mozart showed himself to be brilliant at writing orchestral music and singing parts, as well as putting across comedy and drama. This all-round ability made him one of opera's greatest geniuses.

Above: A scene from Mozart's *The Magic Flute* showing Prince Tamino rescuing Princess Pamina.

opera) style. Back in Vienna Mozart met Christoph Willibald Gluck (1714–1787) and saw his opera *Alceste* when it was performed in 1767. By this time operatic works had generally become overpowered by the music, so that the plots seemed shallow and not very believable. Gluck reformed opera by making the stories simpler and using the music to create the atmosphere. This made a great impression on Mozart, who wrote 22 operas in all.

His last five stand out as his greatest. *The Marriage of Figaro*, written in 1786, is one of the most popular operas of all time. *Don Giovanni* followed in 1787, and *Così fan tutte* ("So do they all") in 1790. These works are all comic masterpieces, whose librettos (or

Left: German composer Christoph Willibald Gluck. His revolutionary operas, which used music to reinforce the plot rather than overpower it, had a great influence on Mozart.

Above: This 19th-century painting shows Mozart composing a Requiem while on his deathbed. He was never to finish the piece.

A prayer for the dying

Most of Mozart's church music was written while he was at the court of Salzburg. He was asked to compose music for the Archbishop's services in Salzburg Cathedral. He had been made court concertmaster in 1769 and wrote masses and **motets**, as well as setting **psalms** to music. But he quarreled with the Archbishop in 1781 and was dismissed.

Mozart then moved permanently to Vienna, where he wrote just three further works for the church. In the last year of his life he began what would have been the greatest of these works—a Requiem, or mass for the souls of the dead.

While writing his Requiem, Mozart suffered from fever and severe head-aches. He became concerned with his own death, and in the end he died—probably of typhus—before he could finish the piece. The Requiem that is performed today was completed by two of Mozart's pupils. Nevertheless it is a work of unsurpassed beauty.

Many rumors about Mozart's death have lasted through the centuries. One is that he was poisoned by the Italian composer Antonio Salieri (1750–1825), who was jealous of him, but there is no real evidence for this. Perhaps, as in other cases where an extraordinary person has died young, people find it hard to accept and search for other reasons. Yet Mozart achieved more than many other composers who lived twice as long, leaving behind more than 600 musical compositions.

A powerful voice emerges

One of the most remarkable figures of the Classical era is Ludwig van Beethoven (1770–1827). When he is mentioned today, most people have a strong image in their minds of a dark, brooding man who wrote passionate

words) were written in Italian by the poet Lorenzo da Ponte (1749–1838). In 1791, the last year of his life, Mozart wrote two operas: *The Magic Flute* and *La clemenza di Tito* ("The clemency of Titus").

One of Mozart's other contributions to opera was that he made the characters in them seem like real people. Before Mozart operatic characters were usually symbolic of a specific type of person, either good or bad, happy or sad, and they remained the same type of person throughout the opera. Mozart's characters, however, have different moods and go through many changes, just as people do in real life. This is why his operas ring true and are still so popular today.

to make him a star like Mozart, made him practice violin and piano for hours on end, beating him when he made too many mistakes. When Beethoven was eight, he played at the court in Bonn, but he was not a big success. The following year he began taking lessons from the court organist Christian Gottlob Neefe (1748–1798) and became a harpsichordist in the court orchestra at the age of 13.

Beethoven was determined to learn music throughout his early life. At 17 he went to study in Vienna, where he was said to have met Mozart, who was very impressed by him and gave him some lessons. A few years later Beethoven's quest for learning led him to move permanently to Vienna, where Haydn agreed to take him on as a pupil. But he did not like Haydn's methods of teaching, which he thought were not thorough enough, and it was a relief to him when Haydn left for London in 1794. Beethoven then studied with a new teacher and later turned to Vienna's leading Italian opera composer, Antonio Salieri, for instruction.

and powerful music. This is close to the truth, since Beethoven did not have an easy life. He struggled with relationships the whole of his life, with money most of his life, and with deafness from relatively early on. Perhaps it was these struggles and his suffering that gave Beethoven's music such enormous depth and drama.

Beethoven was greatly influenced by Haydn and Mozart, but he began to stamp his own mark on the musical world as early as 1800 with his First Symphony. It begins with a powerful discord—a chord that leads the music into an uncomfortable key that creates a feeling of tension. To audiences at the time it was an unacceptable way to start a symphony.

A difficult childhood

Born in Bonn, Germany, in 1770, Beethoven had a life that was difficult from the start. His father, determined

Above: A portrait of Ludwig van Beethoven. Although he was later described as a leading Romantic composer, his early works were much influenced by Bach, Haydn, and Mozart.

Right: Beethoven composes music at his home, surrounded by his books, instruments, and piles of musical manuscripts.

Beethoven and the piano

The piano was truly Beethoven's instrument. He was an excellent and dramatic pianist who, like Mozart, performed his own works to earn money and find new patrons for his composing. As a result, his piano compositions were written for his personal style of playing. At a time when the piano was still being developed as an instrument, the quality and complexity of Beethoven's piano music made it very difficult to play. It became much easier when improvements in the piano's hammer mechanism allowed notes to be repeated more rapidly.

Beethoven's early piano works, including three piano quartets written when he was just a boy, show the influence of C.P.E. Bach, Haydn, and Mozart. Yet the most important of Beethoven's piano works are his 32 piano sonatas, the first of which was dedicated to Haydn. The *Pathétique* ("With Great Emotion") sonata, first performed in 1799, is one of the earliest works to show hints of the new lush, emotional style that was gradually becoming an essential part of Beethoven's music. Indeed, the music of Beethoven, like that of many other composers who came after him, is often described as "romantic." The term refers to music that expressed deep personal emotion and was freer in form than music of the Classical period. Yet although Beethoven's music is deeply emotional, it is always clearly based on Classical ideas of musical form.

Beethoven wrote five great piano concertos, the last of which was completed in 1809. In the last three he continues Mozart's practice of having both the orchestra and the piano play a major role in developing the musical theme. He made them battle with each other to produce a dramatic music in which the conflict is only resolved in the last movement.

Cracking the string quartet

Just as the piano sonata represents the highest point in Beethoven's writing for the keyboard, the string quartet represents the peak of his string compositions. He did not write any

Below: Beethoven conducts one of his string and piano compositions before Count Razumovsky and his family.

Below: The Baroque orchestra (top) was small, with only a few woodwind and brass instruments. The Classical orchestra (bottom) was much larger and featured brass, woodwind, more percussion, and a piano in place of the harpsichord.

string quartets during his early career, admitting that he did not find them easy to compose. However, he continued to study this form of composition with his teacher Johann Georg Albrechtsberger (1736–1809) three times a week for over a year.

Beethoven was 28 before he wrote his first string quartets—a set of six published in 1801. On sending it to a friend, he wrote: "Only now have I learned to write quartets properly." From then on Beethoven began to write string quartets in earnest. His second group of string quartets was a set of three dedicated to Count Razumovsky, the Russian ambassador in Vienna. They have long individual movements and show that Beethoven was developing his own quartet style.

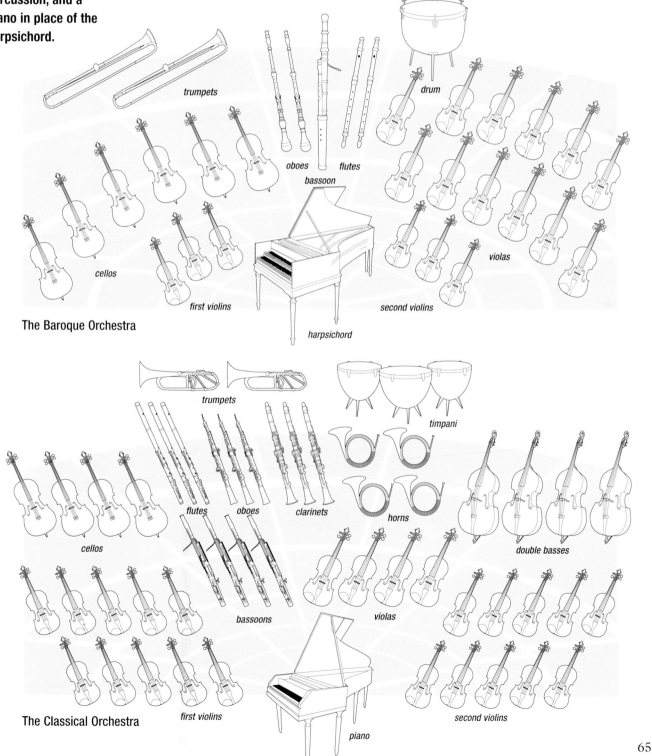

The Baroque Orchestra

trumpets · oboes · flutes · bassoon · drum · cellos · first violins · harpsichord · second violins · violas

The Classical Orchestra

trumpets · flutes · oboes · clarinets · timpani · horns · cellos · double basses · bassoons · violas · first violins · piano · second violins

BEETHOVEN'S NINTH SYMPHONY

Beethoven's ninth and final symphony was first performed in 1823. For the words of the choral finale he used the German poet Schiller's *An die Freude* ("Ode to Joy")—words he had known as far back as 1793.

Beethoven was uncertain about using a choral ending, since voices had never been used in a symphony before. He even considered rewriting the finale with instrumental parts. However, the ending was very powerful and had an emotional effect on the audience. At the end of the symphony's first performance, which Beethoven conducted, the audience stood, cheering and clapping wildly. Beethoven, with his back to the audience, was unaware of their appreciation because of his deafness. A member of the orchestra tugged his sleeve and pointed to the cheering crowd. As Beethoven turned to see them, the audience roared its approval of the magnificent music it had just heard.

It involved using complex musical structures and short themes that were imitated or repeated by different instruments. Beethoven wrote five quartets in his last years, when he was completely deaf, which are of amazing technical mastery and individuality.

Beethoven became very interested in the fugue and variation forms in his later years, and this showed in his string quartets. In 1825 he wrote a long and difficult fugue as the end section to his Quartet in B-flat, Opus 130, and then replaced it with an alternative finale. It was published separately under the title *Grosse Fuge* ("Great Fugue").

First Romantic violin concerto

Beethoven also wrote a beautiful violin concerto, which was performed in 1806. It is regarded as the first Romantic violin concerto because of the imaginative interplay between the orchestra and the solo violinist. He also composed the first concerto for violin, cello, and piano. Using the usual instruments of the string trio, it is known as a triple concerto.

Expanding the orchestra

When Haydn and Mozart were writing their later symphonies, the orchestra stayed more or less the same size. The instruments usually included flutes, oboes, bassoons, horns, strings, and timpani, with occasional trumpets and clarinets (see page 65). However, Beethoven often wrote his orchestral pieces for more instruments to increase the range of sounds. He therefore required more players. The large orchestra he used in his late symphonies became the basis for most orchestras for the remainder of the 19th century.

In his first two symphonies Beethoven used the old Classical orchestra, adding clarinets. In the Third Symphony, the *Eroica* (1804), he used an extra horn. But it was in his Fifth Symphony that he made the first big changes: he used a piccolo, double bassoon, and three trombones, none of which had been heard before in a symphony. Adding these instruments gave the orchestral sound more weight and richness.

Beethoven's symphonies are played more today than those of any other composer

---

In Beethoven's momentous Ninth Symphony (1817–1823), known as the *Choral* Symphony, he again added to the orchestra. Along with piccolo, double bassoon, four horns, and three trombones, there were cymbals, **bass** drum, and triangle in the percussion section. Even more amazing was the addition of soprano, alto, **tenor**, and bass vocal soloists—as well as a full choir. Beethoven's symphonies are probably played more today than those of any other composer.

Above: Isolated by deafness, and often depressed and alone, Beethoven nonetheless "heard" remarkable pieces of music in his head. Many of these pieces are still played and heard today.

BEETHOVEN'S DEAFNESS

As early as 1796, when he was 26 years old, Beethoven noticed the first signs of deafness. Ashamed and embarrassed at his condition, he began to avoid people. Nothing could be done about his loss of hearing, and it became gradually worse. At first he used an ear trumpet, but soon this was useless, and he had to ask people to write down their remarks and questions. By 1815 he had to give up playing music in public because he was completely deaf. It is a great tribute to him that his quality as a composer was not affected by his deafness, and some experts believe that his writing actually became even greater after he lost his hearing.

Nevertheless, Beethoven's general ill-health caused him a great deal of pain and often made him depressed. It also affected his relationships with people, especially since he had a violent temper and was often rude to others. Despite this, he is said to have had a number of close relationships with women, although he never married.

Beethoven's impact

Beethoven stood at the crossroads of the Classical and Romantic eras. In his earliest works he carried on many of the musical forms of his Classical predecessors, such as the three-movement form for the concerto and sonata and the four-movement form for the symphony and string quartet. Yet he was never afraid to adapt and mold these forms to fit his own ideas. Although he only completed one opera, *Fidelio* (1805), it is considered a masterpiece. Throughout his life his work remained rooted in the Classical era, while at the same time it looked forward to the new Romanticism.

Beethoven's many personal sufferings—such as his search for love, which he never found, and his deafness, which took over completely in the end—isolated him from other people. Left to himself, he directed his innermost feelings into the one thing he had control over—his music. These characteristics made Beethoven a perfect example of the Romantic composer—and there would be no 19th-century composer who would be free from his influence.

Above: Beethoven's ear trumpet on top of the manuscript of his *Eroica* Symphony.

TIMELINE

c.41,000 B.C. Musical instruments like flutes are made out of bones, shells, and sticks.

c.10,000 B.C. Andean peoples in South America begin playing wind and percussion instruments.

c.3000 B.C. Egyptians write songs and play flutes, harps, trumpets, tambourines, and drums.

c.2000 B.C. Pentatonic (five-note) scale is developed.

c.1400 B.C. The Chinese play drums, bells, flutes, and chimes.

c.1100 B.C. The Chinese are using the zither and a mouth organ called the *sheng*.

c.550 B.C. Greek philosopher Pythagoras originates the idea of notes, octaves, pitches, and scales.

c.380 B.C. Greek philosophers encourage music education. Instruments include the *kithara* (a lyre) and *aulos* (like an oboe).

c.350 B.C. Greek theorist Aristoxenus identifies rhythm, semitones, and explains scales.

c.300 B.C. Greek engineer Ktesibios invents the organ, using water to control the air pressure.

c.100 A.D. Christians sing hymns and psalms, using a solo-and-response method.

late 500s A.D. Pope Gregory I standardizes church music, known as Gregorian chant, or plainsong.

700s A.D. Moors invade Spain and southern Europe, bringing their instruments, sliding modes, and the origins of flamenco.

c.800 A.D. The Japanese classical music known as *gagaku* begins.

800s A.D. Air pumped through bellows replaces water as the means for working an organ.

900s A.D. Bowed instruments are brought to Europe from Asia.

c.1025 Guido d'Arezzo invents musical notation, including staves.

1000s–1100s Minstrels roam Europe performing secular music.

1100s Organum music leads to the more complex, multiple-part music known as polyphony.

late 1100s Drums become a common rhythm-keeping instrument in Europe.

1200s In France composers adapt plainsong to invent the motet—a form of vocal polyphonic music.

1300s A system of harmony develops out of plainsong in France and Italy.

early 1300s Persian Amir Khusrau creates Indian classical music, Sufi *qawwali* music, and the sitar.

1400s The slide trombone is developed.

1476 The first music books of plainsong are printed.

c.1500 Muslims invade Indonesia and note that gamelan music has been around for centuries.

1500s The French chanson (song) becomes popular—it often told a story of lost love.

Italian musicians begin writing original music and introduce dynamics and orchestration.

In England Thomas Tallis writes many anthems, which become an important musical form.

In the Lutheran church the congregation joins in the singing, and hymns are in the local language (rather than Latin).

1501 Ottaviano dei Petrucci publishes the first book of polyphonic music.

c.1550s The first *son* song is performed in Santiago, Chile.

1558 Italian composer Gioseffo Zarlino publishes *Le istitutioni harmoniche,* which describes the use of chords in writing harmony.

late 1500s Music appears with specific parts for female singers.

Nicola Vincentino begins writing madrigals—songs for several unaccompanied voices.

1594 Jacopo Peri composes *Dafne,* the first opera.

1597 English composer John Dowland publishes four books of songs with lute accompaniment.

1600 Dawn of the Baroque era.

1600s African slaves are brought to Europe and America, bringing their music with them.

Oratorios start to develop at religious meetings held by the Italian Filippo Neri.

Castrati are singing in operas.

1620 Pilgrims arrive in America from Europe bringing their psalms and hymns with them.

1685 Johann Sebastian Bach born in Germany.

1689 The English opera *Dido and Aeneas* by Henry Purcell opens in London.

early 1700s Johann Christoff Denner invents the clarinet.

1709 Bartolomeo Cristofori invents the pianoforte (the piano).

1722 Bach publishes *The Well-tempered Clavichord,* a collection of keyboard pieces in all the major and minor keys.

1727 The first German singspiel (*The Devil Is Loose*) is produced.

1731 The first formal classical concert takes place in America.

1742 The first performance of Handel's oratorio *Messiah.*

1748 The first public concert hall opens in Oxford, England.

c.1750 The Classical era begins.

1756 Wolfgang Amadeus Mozart born in Salzburg, Austria.

1770 William Billings publishes the first book of American music, *The New-England Psalm-Singer.*

Ludwig van Beethoven born in Bonn, Germany.

1777 "Yankee Doodle" is the first American song published in Europe.

1786 Mozart composes his opera *The Marriage of Figaro.*

late 1700s German composers start writing lieder, songs in which the lyrics are all-important.

1790 The first performance of Peking (Beijing) opera.

1791–1795 "Father of the symphony" Joseph Haydn writes his 12 "London" symphonies, including his *Surprise* Symphony.

c.1800 Beethoven increases the size of the classical orchestra and ushers in the Romantic era.

The waltz grows in popularity throughout Europe.

1800s African-American slaves use Christian hymns as the basis for their own spirituals.

early 1800s Caribbean and African styles combine in Sierra Leone to create "highlife."

1814 "The Star-Spangled Banner" is first performed.

1823 Beethoven completes his Ninth Symphony.

mid-1840s Blackfaced minstrel shows become popular in America and Britain.

1853 First performance of Verdi's opera *La Traviata.*

c.1850s The banjo becomes a popular instrument among gold miners in America.

European composers start writing nationalistic music.

c.1860 Vienna, Austria, becomes the main center of operetta.

1864 Adolphe Sax invents the saxophone.

1871 Spirituals are first performed for a white audience by the Jubilee Singers.

1876 Brahms completes his First Symphony.

First performance of Wagner's four-opera cycle *The Ring of the Nibelungen.*

1877 First performance of Tchaikovsky's ballet *Swan Lake.*

1878 David Edward Hughes invents the carbon microphone.

1879 Bandleader Miguel Failde creates *danzón* dance music.

late 1800s Appalachian folk music is adapted into hillbilly—and later country—music.

Barbershop quartet singing becomes popular in America.

Millions of copies of sheet music are sold for people to play songs on their pianos at home.

African Americans start performing the blues.

c.1890 Vaudeville becomes America's most popular form of mass entertainment.

1891 Carnegie Hall opens in New York City.

1894 First performance of the impressionist *Prélude à l'après-midi d'un faune* by Debussy.

Emil Berliner invents the gramophone and the record disk.

1896 First performance of Puccini's opera *La Bohème.*

1899 Scott Joplin's "Maple Leaf Rag" helps make ragtime popular.

c.1900 Expressionist composers begin placing equal importance on all 12 semitones of the scale.

Mariachi bands begin performing in Mexico.

early 1900s In New Orleans African-American marching bands form the first jazz groups.

African Americans adapt "shout" songs and church "witness" rituals to make gospel.

Austrian composers Arnold Schoenberg and Alban Berg develop *Sprechgesang* singing.

1901 Premiere of Rachmaninov's Second Piano Concerto.

1902 Enrico Caruso makes recordings for the gramophone.

1906 Béla Bartók begins recording Hungarian folk songs.

1909 William Ludwig invents the foot pedal for the bass drum.

c.1910 Tin Pan Alley starts producing popular songs.

1911 Premiere of Richard Strauss's opera *Der Rosenkavalier*.

1913 First performance in Paris of Stravinsky's *The Rite of Spring* causes a riot in the audience.

1917 The Original Dixieland Jazz Band makes the first phonograph recordings of jazz tunes.

1920 Léon Thérémin invents the "theremin," the first important electronic instrument.

Mamie Smith's "Crazy Blues" is the first blues recording featuring a black performer.

1920–1923 Arnold Schoenberg writes his first pieces of serialist music, based on a tone row.

1920s The jazz age. Chicago replaces New Orleans as the center of jazz.

The first jug bands are formed.

The beginnings of electronic music.

Enka, combining Western music with traditional Japanese minor modes, develops in Japan.

Blues guitarists develop the slide technique of gliding the fingers up and down the strings instead of using the frets.

The amplifier is invented.

The tango becomes popular in America and Europe.

Dance-band singers start using the microphone.

Blues musicians start playing a "walking bass," which leads to boogie-woogie.

Muzak begins recording production (background) music.

Sheet-music sales decrease as record sales increase.

1921 Prokofiev's opera *The Love for Three Oranges* first performed.

1923 King Oliver's Creole Jazz Band, featuring Louis Armstrong on trumpet, makes the first jazz

recordings by an all-black group.

The first country record, Fiddlin' John Carson's "The Little Old Log Cabin in the Lane," is made in Atlanta, Georgia.

1924 Premiere of George Gershwin's *Rhapsody in Blue*.

1925 George Dewey Hay begins broadcasting a radio show—later known as *The Grand Ole Opry*—from Nashville, Tennessee.

1926 Louis Armstrong invents "scat singing."

1927 Premiere of the first modern musical—Jerome Kern and Oscar Hammerstein II's *Show Boat*.

The first motion picture with sound is *The Jazz Singer*.

1928 Joe Falcon's "Allons a Lafayette" is the first Cajun record.

Kurt Weill and Bertolt Brecht's musical *The Threepenny Opera* includes political satire.

1930s "Swing"—African-American dance music—becomes popular.

Folk singer Woody Guthrie sings songs about the Depression.

1934 The Hammond organ is invented by Laurens Hammond.

Magnetic recording tape is developed.

1935 The electric guitar and the tape recorder are invented.

1938 Mambo music begins in Cuba.

1940s Latin music begins to influence American jazz.

Big-band singers Ella Fitzgerald, Peggy Lee, and Frank Sinatra embark on solo careers.

Bebop emerges as improvisational jazz music.

1943–1959 Rodgers and Hammerstein write a string of successful musicals.

1944 Premiere of Aaron Copland's ballet *Appalachian Spring*.

late 1940s Dance "race music" becomes "rhythm and blues."

Musique concrète is used in orchestral compositions.

The electric piano is invented.

1948 The long-playing 33⅓ record (the LP) is introduced.

1949 "Father of honky-tonk" Hank Williams has first big hit with "Lovesick Blues."

Miles Davis releases *Birth of the Cool*, the first "cool jazz" record.

1950s Leo Fender designs the Telecaster and the Stratocaster electric guitars.

A new music called bossa nova emerges from Brazil—a light jazz sound with samba and *choro* influences.

Young African Americans start singing doo-wop.

"Soul" emerges, adapted from the gospel sound.

Technological advances include tape recording and stereo.

1951 Elliot Carter composes his atonal String Quartet No. 1.

1952 Pierre Boulez composes his serialist piece *Structures I*.

John Cage performs his experimental piece *4' 33"*.

1953 Enrique Jorrin invents the cha-cha-cha.

mid-1950s DJ Alan Freed coins the term "rock 'n' roll."

1955 The first synthesizer is built.

1956 Elvis Presley reaches No. 1 with the rock 'n' roll song "Heartbreak Hotel."

Frank Sinatra releases *Songs for Swinging Lovers*.

1959 Stockhausen performs his aleatory piece *Zyklus*.

Miles Davis abandons cool in favor of modal jazz.

Rock 'n' roll star Buddy Holly is killed in a place crash.

Berry Gordy and Smokey Robinson start Motown Records.

1960 The Shirelles become the first black girl group to have a No. 1 hit single.

Saxophonist Ornette Coleman starts a new improvisational jazz sound called "free jazz."

1960s Period performances of Baroque pieces become popular.

The Andean music known as *chicha* is developed.

1962 The Beatles make their first record, "Love Me Do."

1963 "Queen of Country" Patsy Cline dies in a plane crash.

Bob Dylan records the 1960s folk anthem "Blowin' in the Wind."

1965 James Brown introduces a new style of dance music, "funk."

Folk rock begins when Bob Dylan plays an electric guitar instead of an acoustic one at the Newport Jazz Festival.

The analog synthesizer is made available to the public.

late 1960s Some bands begin playing psychedelic rock.

Progressive rock emerges.

1967 Digital recording technology is developed.

The Beatles release *Sgt. Pepper's Lonely Hearts Club Band*.

1968 Steppenwolf's "Born to Be Wild" is first heavy metal record.

Country singer Johnny Cash releases *Live at Folsom Prison*.

1969 Miles Davis combines free jazz and rock to form "fusion."

1970s Indian music becomes popular in the West.

Salsa becomes a popular type of Latin-based dance music.

Jamaica's reggae begins to spread around the world.

mid-1970s Disco music becomes popular.

1976 Punk rock band the Sex Pistols sends shock waves across Britain with "Anarchy in the U.K."

late 1970s The DJ-led hip-hop begins among the black urban youth of America.

1979 Ry Cooder's album *Bop till You Drop* is the first to use a digital multitrack system.

1980s Cajun music enjoys a national revival.

Digital recording becomes available.

The introduction of CDs transforms the music industry.

1981 MTV begins broadcasting on cable and satellite.

1983 MIDI (Musical Instrument Digital Interface) enables two or more electronic instruments to communicate with each other.

1986 Ladysmith Black Mambazo from South Africa introduces Zulu a capella music to the world.

1987 Premiere of John Adams' minimalist opera *Nixon in China*.

1990s Digital sampling becomes more common in pop music.

1996 In the violent world of gangsta rap, Tupac Shakur is shot dead in Las Vegas.

late 1990s Hospitals and clinics begin using music therapy.

Internet users begin downloading music onto their personal computers.

Glossary

air A song, melody, or tune.

allemande A German dance in 3/4 time (counted as 1-2-3, 1-2-3), which later became a dance form in 2/4 time (counted as 1-2, 1-2). Composers often used it as a section within a suite.

alto The lowest female singing voice, or a high male voice.

anthem Originally a Protestant vocal piece with religious words, which soon developed into a short song written in English with either moral or religious lyrics and a powerful chorus. There are two types of anthems. The full anthem is sung by a choir. The verse anthem starts with a verse sung by a soloist, accompanied by an instrument, that is followed by a chorus sung by a choir.

antiphonal When separate groups of performers alternate or respond to each other musically.

arrangement A musical composition that is rewritten or adapted for different instruments.

ballad At first it was a song that accompanied dancing; it later became either a song telling a story or a slow, sentimental song.

bass The lowest male singing voice, the lowest-sounding part of a musical composition, or the lowest-sounding instrument of a family of instruments, such as the bass drum, double bass, bass clarinet, etc.

cantata A vocal composition in several movements for soloists and a chorus, accompanied by an orchestra.

choir An organized group of singers, usually of church music.

chorale A hymn or song based on a traditional or composed melody that is sung by a choir, usually in church.

chord Three or more notes that are sounded at the same time.

chorus An organized group of singers, usually of nonchurch music, or the section of a song that comes after the verse and is usually repeated again at the end of each verse.

chromatic Either a series of notes moving in half-tones (semitones) or notes that appear in a musical work that are not notes of the main keys used in the composition.

concerto At first it was a composition for voices and a group of instruments, at which time it was called a concerto grosso. Later it became a purely instrumental composition for a solo instrument and an orchestra.

conductor A person who directs the performers by making gestures that mark the tempo, dynamics, and rhythm of the music.

consonance A combination of notes that produces a feeling of harmony and well-being in the listener. Early composers believed that only the intervals of the fourth, fifth, and octave achieved this, but later composers thought the third and sixth intervals also had this effect.

courante A 16th-century French dance in 3/4 time (counted as 1-2-3, 1-2-3) that later became a dance form used in a suite.

duet A musical composition written for two performers.

dynamics Instructions given to the performers of a composition that show how loud or soft the composer intended the music to be played or sung. These instructions can be marked on the music manuscript, as well as indicated by a conductor through his or her gestures.

folk music Music from a specific region or country that is passed down from generation to generation.

frequency The measure of the pitch of a note according to the number of vibrations it gives off in a second.

fugue A piece or movement for two or more parts in which the opening melody is taken up by every part in turn.

harmony Two or more notes sounding together in a "harmonious," or complementary, way.

hymn A song of praise to God, usually written for church services.

improvise/improvisation Creating music spontaneously, without previous thought to what is going to be played or sung, instead of playing the exact notes written in a composition.

incantation Words that are spoken in a steady rhythm to create a powerful or hypnotizing effect.

instrumentation The choice of specific instruments for a musical composition.

interval The distance in pitch between two notes.

key The home scale of a musical composition. Also the part of the keyboard depressed by the fingers.

lyrics The words of a song or piece.

melody A series of notes with a distinct musical shape (also called a tune).

minuet A French country dance in 3/4 time (counted as 1-2-3, 1-2-3) that was also often used as a musical form for the third movement of a symphony, suite, or other Classical composition.

mode One of a series of scales used in medieval times that are still in use in some modern forms of music, such as **folk** and jazz. Modes were adopted by the Christian church from the ancient Greeks. Some of the most common modes in Western music are the Phrygian, the Dorian, and the Ionian.

modulation Changing from one **key** to another in a musical composition.

motet In the early Renaissance it was a musical composition written for the church service for three unaccompanied voices. It used a previously existing plainsong text and **melody** for the lower voice and a different text for the upper voices. Later it became an entirely original composition for many voices, all the **parts** of which were set to the same text, and was often accompanied by instruments.

movement A self-contained section within a larger musical composition.

notation A system of writing down music for others to learn and perform.

note A single sound of a given **pitch**.

octave The eighth **note** up or down from any other note. Also the **interval** between these two notes.

oratorio A dramatic choral composition, usually with religious text and accompanied by instruments. It is similar to an opera, but is performed without acting, costumes, or scenery.

orchestration In a musical composition the assigning of **parts** to specific instruments of an orchestra.

organum A medieval **polyphonic** type of music that used a plainsong **melody** as the main melody and added other **parts** in parallel intervals below it to create **harmony**. In the late Middle Ages composers freed up the harmony in organum by adding parts that could rise above or below the main melody.

overture Either an instrumental composition that is used to introduce a ballet, opera, or **oratorio**, or an independent composition that is often used to open a concert.

part A line of music that is sung by a singer or played by a musician.

pick A small, thin object made of a strong but flexible material that is held between the fingers to pluck the strings of an instrument and create a sound.

piece A musical composition.

pitch The sound quality of a **note**, whether high or low, that is determined by the **frequency** of the vibrations producing the note.

plainsong A style of unaccompanied unison singing associated with the medieval Christian church. Also known as Gregorian chant and plainchant.

polyphony/polyphonic Combining two or more **melodies** or sounds.

prelude The first section of a large-scale musical composition, or a short, independent composition.

psalm A religious song based on the text of the *Book of Psalms* in the Bible.

rhythm/rhythmic The underlying pulse or beat of the music.

rondo A specific musical form with a repeated musical **theme** that alternates with other musical themes.

sarabande A lively 16th-century dance that in the 17th and 18th centuries became a slow and stately dance in 3/4 time (counted as 1-2-3, 1-2-3), as well as a musical form that composers used as a section within a **suite**.

scale A series of (usually) eight **notes** ascending or descending in alphabetical order and in specified intervals (whole-tones or half-tones).

secular Music that is nonreligious and not written for the church.

semitone One of the 12 half-tones in an **octave**.

sight-singing Singing a piece of music at first sight without previous rehearsal by reading the musical **notes**, words, signs, and directions that are written down on paper.

singspiel A German opera with some spoken dialogue.

suite An instrumental composition made up of short sections or **movements** that usually include dance forms such as the **allemande**, **courante**, **minuet**, and **sarabande**.

tempo The speed at which a musical **piece** is played, whether fast or slow.

tenor In early **polyphonic** music it meant the low voice that carried the **melody**. It also means the highest normal adult male singing voice, or an instrument with a range similar to the tenor voice, such as the tenor saxophone or the tenor horn.

theme The main musical idea, subject, or **melody** of a composition.

time signature The sign, such as 2/4 (counted 1-2, 1-2), 3/4 (counted 1-2-3, 1-2-3), or 4/4 (counted 1-2-3-4, 1-2-3-4), that is placed at the beginning of a musical composition to indicate how many beats to the bar (measure) and of what value (e.g., quarter-note).

tone color The sound quality of a voice or instrument.

trio A group of three performers, a composition for three performers, or the middle section of a **minuet**.

Musical Notation

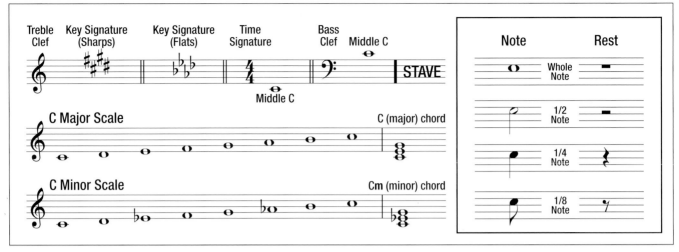

Further Reading

Barber, David W., with Dave Donald (illustrator). *Bach, Beethoven, and the Boys.* Buffalo, NY: Barron's Juveniles, 1999.

Bergamini, Andrea, with Manuela Cappon (illustrator). *Beethoven and the Classical Age.* Hauppage, NY: Barron's Juveniles, 1999.

Bergamini, Andrea. *Music of the World* (Masters of Music). Hauppage, NY: Barron's Juveniles, 1999.

Book for Young Musicians, The. New York: Shooting Star Press, 1996.

Catucci, Stefano, and Hans Tid, with Sergio and Giampaolo Faleschini (illustrators). *Bach and Baroque Music* (Masters of Music). Hauppage, NY: Barron's Juveniles, 1998.

Cosman, Madeleine Pelner. *Medieval Baker's Daughter: A Bilingual Adventure in Medieval Life with Costumes, Banners, Music, Food, and a Mystery Play.* New York: Bard Hall Press, 1984.

Danes, Emma. *Music Theory for Beginners.* Tulsa, OK: EDC Publications, 1997.

Gatti, Anne, with Peter Malone (illustrator). *The Magic Flute.* San Francisco: Chronicle Books, 1997.

Hammond, Susan. *Classical Kids: Hallelujah, Handel!* Ontario, Canada: The Children's Group, 1995.

Hammond, Susan. *Classical Kids: Vivaldi's Ring of Mystery.* Ontario, Canada: The Children's Group, 1995.

Krull, Kathleen, with Kathryn Hewitt (illustrator). *Lives of the Musicians: Good Times, Bad Times (And What the Neighbors Thought).* New York: Harcourt Brace, 1993.

Langley, Andrew, and Andy Crawford. *Renaissance.* New York: Knopf, 1999.

Ludwig, Charles, with Arthur Schneider (illustrator). *George Frideric Handel, Composer of Messiah.* Milford, MI: Mott Media, 1987.

Manniche, Lise. *Musical Instruments from the Tomb of Tutankhamun.* Oakville, CT: David Brown Book Company, 1976.

Mason, Antony, with Richard Berridge (illustrator). *Medieval Times* (If You Were There). New York: Simon & Schuster, 1996.

McLeish, Kenneth, and Valerie McLeish. *Oxford First Companion to Composers and Their Music.* Oxford: Oxford University Press, 1982.

Music and Sound (Modern Media Series). Hauppage, NY: Barron's Educational Series, 2000.

Patton, Barbara W., with Leslie Patton (illustrator). *Introducing Johann Sebastian Bach* (Introducing the Composers). Sunnyvale, CA: Soundboard Books, 1992.

Patton, Barbara W. *Introducing Wolfgang Amadeus Mozart* (Introducing the Composers). Sunnyvale, CA: Soundboard Books, 1991.

Pogue, David, and Scott Speck. *Classical Music for Dummies.* Foster City, CA: IDG Books, 1997.

Sabin, Louis, with Ellen Beier (illustrator). *Ludwig van Beethoven: Young Composer.* Mahwah, NY: Troll Association, 1992.

Salvi, Francesco, and Hans Tid, with L.R. Galante and Manuela Cappon (illustrators). *Mozart and Classical Music* (Masters of Music). Hauppage, NY: Barron's Juveniles, 1998.

Taylor, Barbara. *Hear! Hear!* New York: Random House, 1991.

Venezia, Mike. *Ludwig van Beethoven.* New York: Children's Press, 1996.

Useful websites

A History of Ancient Greek Music (covering the major periods in Greek musical history)
http://w4u.eexi.gr/~gymfil/brown

Baroque Music (includes biographies of all major Baroque composers)
http://www.islandnet.com/~arton/baroqmus.html

The Capistrano School (an educational site that contains Classical reference material)
http://www.empire.k12.ca.us/capistrano/Capistra.htm

Eras Online: Middle Ages (major musical trends in the medieval world)
http://www.essentialsofmusic.com/eras/medieval.html

Eras Online: Renaissance (major musical trends in the Renaissance era)
http://www.essentialsofmusic.com/eras/renaissance.html

The Internet Renaissance Band (includes downloadable clips of Renaissance music)
http://www.csupomona.edu/~jcclark/emusic/index.html

Music History 102 (music from the Middle Ages to the present day)
http://www.ipl.org/exhibit/mushist

Note Reading (the basics of reading music)
http://library.thinkquest.org/15413/theory/note-reading.htm

Set Index

Numbers in **bold type** are volume numbers.

Page numbers in *italics* refer to picture captions or a caption and text reference on the same page.

A

A&R executives **8**:45–46
Aboriginal music **9**:*29*
Abshire, Nathan **4**:*64–65*
Academy of Ancient Music **2**:*67*
a cappella **2**:28, **4**:5, **10**:61–63
accents **1**:33
accordion **3**:21–22, **4**:*63*, 64–65
acid house **6**:65, **9**:51
Acis and Galatea (Handel) **10**:*20*
acoustics **8**:5
Acuff, Roy **4**:41, 49
Adams, John **2**:61, **10**:35
ADAT recording **8**:*60*, **9**:64
Adderley, "Cannonball" **5**:62, 63
Adé, King Sunny **3**:*60*
Aerosmith **5**:38, **6**:36
Afghanistan **3**:*49*
Africa **3**:58–67, **10**:*4*, 56, *58*, 61–63
"Afro-Beat" **3**:*62*
Afro-Cubans, the **3**:13
agago **3**:27
agents **8**:42
Aguilera, Christina **6**:66
aguinaldo **3**:11
Ainsworth Psalter **4**:5–6
Akhnaten (Glass) **10**:35
Aladdin Laddies **4**:48
Albee, Edward F. **7**:*14*
Albéniz, Isaac **2**:29
albums, record **8**:*36*, 37
Alcina (Handel) **10**:*23*
aleatory music **2**:59
al-jil **3**:56
Allen, Rex **4**:44
Allen, Richard **5**:12
Allison, Jerry **6**:14
Allsop, Tommy **6**:15
Almanac Singers **4**:24
Alonso, Pacho **3**:14
alt.country **4**:61
alternative music **6**:43–45
altos **10**:42
amateur musicians **8**:14–15
Amati family **9**:*07*
America
   early music **4**:4–17
   See also United States
American Bandstand **6**:*20*
American Folk Blues Festival **5**:*37*
Ames, Roger **8**:*50*
Amharic music **3**:57
Ammons, Albert **5**:49
Amos, Tori **6**:66
amplification **9**:39–40
analog recording **9**:62
andaluz **3**:55
Andean music **3**:23–25
Anderson, Bill **4**:49
Andrews, Julie **7**:*39*
Angels, the **6**:18
Animals, the **5**:37
Annie Get Your Gun (Berlin) **7**:*37*

antara **3**:23–24
anthems **1**:24–25, 40, **4**:9, 11
antiphonal music **1**:30
Appalachian Mountains **4**:19–20, 36, 39
Aquinas, Thomas **8**:7
Arawak Indians **3**:5
Arban, Joseph **8**:11
Arcano, Antonio **3**:12
Ardoin, Amédée **4**:64
Arezzo, Guido d' **1**:16, 23, **10**:40–*41*
Argentina **3**:30–31
arias **1**:34
Aristotle **1**:8, **8**:5–6
Aristoxenus **1**:10–11, **8**:6
Arlen, Harold **7**:35, 38
armonicas **4**:8
Armstrong, Louis **5**:25, *43*, 44, 45, 46, 47, 54–55
Arnold, Eddy **4**:49
arrangements **1**:26
arribeño **3**:23
Arrow **3**:41
Arroyo, Joe **3**:*19*
Ars Nova **1**:16, 17
Art Ensemble of Chicago **5**:64
ASCAP **7**:21, **8**:33
Atkins, Chet **4**:48
Atlantic Records label **6**:*47–49*, **8**:48
atonal music **2**:36, 37, 39, 60, **10**:64
audio architecture **7**:67
Audion tubes **9**:43
Augustine, St. **8**:6–7, **10**:*40*
aulos **1**:8, 9, **10**:38–39
Auric, Georges **2**:44
Australia **9**:27
authentic performances **2**:65–66, 67, **10**:37
autoharp **4**:39
Autry, Gene **4**:40, *44*
avant-garde music **5**:63, 67, **9**:46
Aweke, Aster **3**:57
Aznavour, Charles **7**:23

B

Bacharach, Burt **5**:19, **7**:42, **10**:54–55
Bach dynasty **1**:45–49
   Bach, C.P.E. **1**:49, 51–53, **9**:*36*
   Bach, J.C. **1**:49, 58, 59–60, **9**:*36*
   Bach, J.S. **1**:45, 46–49, **2**:62–63, 64, **9**:10, *36*, **10**:42
background music **7**:67
backing singers **8**:19–20
Backstreet Boys **6**:66
Baez, Joan **4**:28–29, *30*, 34
bagpipes **9**:*30*
Bahamas **3**:33, 38–*39*
Bailey, Mildred **5**:56
bajo **4**:53
Baker, LaVerne **6**:7
Bakersfield **4**:54, 55, 56
Bali **3**:*50*, 51

ballads **1**:18, **4**:5, 18, 19, 24, **5**:21–22
ballates **1**:25
ballet de cour **1**:35
ballet music **2**:*17*–19, 40, 41, 45, 46, 52, 53, 64
Bambaata, DJ Afrika **6**:58, 60
bambola **3**:22
banda **3**:22
bandola **3**:30
bandoneón **3**:31, **5**:67
banduría **3**:30
bandurria **3**:9
bania **4**:39
Banister, John **1**:42
banjo **4**:*12*, 13, *18*, 20, *39*, **5**:5, 7, **9**:*16*
Banton, Buju **3**:38
Barbados **3**:33
bar bands **8**:15
bards **1**:18
baritones **10**:9, 37
barn dances **4**:*8*, *19*, 67
Baroque music **1**:32–49, 52, 65, **2**:47, *62*
   revival **2**:62–66, 67
barrelhouse blues **5**:14
Barron, Louis and Bebe **7**:57
Barry, John **7**:62
Bart, Lionel **7**:42
Bartered Bride, The (Smetana) **2**:*23*
Bartók, Béla **2**:43–44, **10**:19
Basie, W. "Count" **5**:51–52
basses, operatic **10**:9, 37, 42
basso continuo part **1**:32
bassoon **9**:*21*, 22
Bauzá, Mario **3**:*13*, 14
Bay Psalm Book, The **4**:6
Bayreuth **2**:16, **10**:*33*, 34
Beach Boys **6**:23, 24–25
Beale St. (Memphis) **5**:20, 30
Beastie Boys **6**:60–61
Beatles **5**:18, **6**:21, *22*, 27, **7**:66, **8**:56
   movies **7**:40, *60*, 61
   Sgt. Pepper's Lonely Hearts Club Band **6**:27–28, **8**:37, 56
BeauSoleil **4**:67
bebop (bop) **5**:56–59, 61
Bechet, Sidney **5**:44, 50
Beck, Jeff **6**:31, **10**:66
Beecham, Thomas **2**:54–55
Beethoven, Ludwig van **1**:53, 62–*67*, **2**:4, 5, **7**:6, **9**:*36*
   symphonies **1**:52, 66, **2**:5, 12, 13, **10**:43–44
Beggar's Opera, The (Pepusch) **7**:5
Beissel, Johann Conrad **4**:7
Belafonte, Harry **3**:*41*
bel canto **1**:38, **10**:24–25, 26
Belen **3**:26
Bellini Quartet **10**:26–27
Bellini, V. **10**:26, *27*
belly-dancing **3**:56
Benedictines **1**:13
Bennett, Tony **4**:46, **6**:65, **10**:52, *54*

"bent" notes **5**:21, 22
Berbers **3**:55
Berg, Alban **2**:*37*, *38*–39, **10**:35, 63
Berio, Luciano **2**:57, **10**:64–65
Berkeley, Busby **7**:*35*
Berlin **1**:*53*, **7**:24–25
Berliner, Emile **8**:47, **9**:55
Berlin, Irving **7**:20, 30, 35–36, *37*, 61, **10**:*48*
Berlin Philharmonic **2**:55
Berlioz, Hector **2**:29, **10**:31, 33
Bernstein, Elmer **7**:56
Bernstein, Leonard **7**:41, **8**:18, *19*
Berry, Chuck **6**:*7*–8, 14
Berry, Ken **8**:*50*
Berwald, Franz **2**:29
bhangra **3**:46, *47*
Bhosle, Asha **3**:46
Bible **1**:6, 12–13, **10**:39
big bands **5**:46, 50–54
   See also swing
Big Bopper **6**:14, *15*
biguine **3**:35–36
Big Youth **3**:38
Bikel, Theodore **4**:31
Billboard (magazine) **10**:*48*
Billings, William **4**:*9*
Bill Haley and the Comets **6**:10, **10**:*48*
Bill Peer's Melody Boys **4**:*51*
Billy Budd (Britten) **10**:35
Binchois, Gilles de Bins dit **1**:24
Bizet, Georges **2**:29, **10**:*32*
Björk **6**:66
Blackboard Jungle, The **6**:10
Black Crowes **5**:38
Black Flag **6**:43
Black Sabbath **5**:38, **6**:35–36
Blackwell, Scrapper **5**:31
Blades, Rubén **3**:*15*
Blakey, Art **5**:57, 61, 62, 63
Bland, James A. **4**:14, **5**:9
Blige, Mary J. **6**:63, 67
Blind Blake **8**:47
Blind Faith **6**:31
Blondie **6**:41–42
Blondy, Alpha **3**:60
Blue Angel, The **7**:*24*, 25
bluegrass **4**:39, 40–42
Blue Grass Boys **4**:41–*42*, *43*
Blue Note label **5**:63, **8**:47, 48, *49*
blues **5**:7, 20–39
   Chicago **5**:31, 34–36, **6**:5
   jump/electric **6**:5
   southern country **6**:10
   See also rhythm and blues
Bluesbreakers **5**:38–39
blues progressions **5**:21
BMI **8**:33
Bobettes **6**:18
Bob Wills and His Texas Playboys **4**:*47*, 48
Bock, Jerry **7**:42
Boehm, Theobold **9**:*19*, 20
Bohemia, nationalist composers

73

2:22–23, 24
Böhm, Georg 1:47
Bolan, Marc 6:37
Bolden, Buddy 5:43, 66
Boléro (Ravel) 2:33–34
Bolivia 3:25
Bollywood 3:46, 47
bomba 3:10, 11, 18
bones 1:4, 5:8, 9:19
Bono 6:42
bon odori festivals 3:52
boogie-woogie 4:48, 5:27, 32, 48–49
Boogie-Woogie Trio 5:49
Booker T. and the MGs 6:48–49
Boone, Pat 6:6–7
bop *See* bebop
Borodin, Alexander 2:26
bossa nova 3:28–29
Boston, music schools 8:10–11, 12, 13
Boston Symphony Orchestra 4:17
Bottle Rockets 4:61
Boubil, Alain 7:47–48
Bouka Guinee 3:35
Boukman Eksperyans 3:35
Boulez, Pierre 2:37, 57
Bowie, David 6:37
boy bands 6:66, 8:56
Brahms, Johannes 2:13–15, 63–64, 10:18
brass instruments 1:9, 2:67, 9:24–31
Brazil 3:26–30
break beats 6:58
breaks 5:43
Brel, Jacques 7:24
Brenston, Jackie 6:5, 32
Briggs, Arthur 5:49
Brill Building 8:29, 30
Bristow, G.F. 4:10, 11
Britten, Benjamin 2:47–48, 10:19, 35, 36, 45
Britton, Thomas 1:42
Broadcast Music Incorporated 7:21
Brook, Michael 3:48
Brooks, Garth 4:58, 59, 60, 61
Broonzy, "Big" Bill 5:26, 31, 36, 6:10
Broschi, Carlo 1:38
Brown, James 3:62, 63, 5:17, 6:52–53, 54
Brown, Milton 4:47–48
Brown, Willie 5:24, 26–27
Brubeck, Dave 5:60, 62
Bruckner, Anton 2:13
Buckersfield 4:54, 56
Bucucos, Los 3:14
Buena Vista Social Club 3:18
Bulgaria 10:60–61
Bülow, Hans von 2:15
bum-bun 3:12
Burgie, Irving 3:41
"Burgundian school" 1:24
Burke, Solomon 6:47, 48
Burleigh, Harry T. 5:11
Butterfield Blues Band 5:39
Butterfield, Paul 5:39
Buxtehude, Dietrich 1:47
Buzzcocks 6:41
Byrds 4:31, 32, 60
Byrd, William 1:25, 26
Byrne, David 3:15, 28

C

cabaret 7:20–27
Cabaret 7:24, 25, 42–43
cabaza 3:8
Caccini, Giulio 1:34, 10:17
cadence music 3:36
cadences 1:22
Cage, John 2:57–58, 59, 10:64
cajones 3:7–8
Cajun music 4:62–67
cakewalk 5:6
Caldwell, Sarah 8:18
California, the blues 5:31–32

call-and-response 4:20, 5:7, 22, 6:49, 10:61
and jazz 5:42, 51
and salsa 3:7, 9–10
Callas, Maria 10:5, 37
call-call-response 5:21
Calloway, Cab 3:13, 5:52
calypso 3:32, 39–41
Camerata 1:33–34, 10:16–17, 21
Campbell, Glen 4:55, 56
can-can 7:22
Candido 5:57
canons 4:9
cantatas 1:31, 45
canto a lo pueta 3:30
Cantor, Eddie 7:17–18
cantu 3:25
cantus firmus 1:31
Capirola, Vincenzo 1:27
Capitol label 5:32
careers, in music 8:14–27
Carey, Mariah 6:65
Caribbean 3:32–41
See also salsa
Carlos, Walter 9:50
Carmen (Bizet) 10:32, 33
Carmina Burana (Orff) 10:44, 45
Carnaval 3:27, 28
Carnegie, Andrew 4:16
Carnegie Hall 4:16, 17
Carpenter, Mary Chapin 4:59, 67
Carreras, José 10:28
Carr, Leroy 5:31
Carson, Fiddlin' John 4:37
Carter, Benny 5:49, 66
Carter, Elliot 2:59–60
Carter Family 4:38–39
Caruso, Enrico 8:46, 47, 10:8–9, 37
Casals, Pablo 9:10
casas de la trova 3:17–18
Cash, Johnny 4:50, 54, 57, 6:10, 12
cassettes 8:65, 9:65, 66
castanets 3:55
castrati 1:38, 10:15–16, 22–23, 24–25
Cavalli, Francesco 1:35
cavaquinho 3:27
CDs *See* compact disks
celempung 3:51
cello 9:6, 10
chacarera 3:31
cha-cha-cha 3:12, 13
Chaliapin, Fyodor 2:27, 10:9
chamame 3:31
chamber music 1:55, 8:17, 9:12
Chandler, Chas 6:32
Chandos anthems 1:40
chansons 1:18, 24, 7:23, 10:13
chansons de geste 10:12
chant, Gregorian
See plainsong/plainchant
Chantels 6:18
chanteymen 4:18
chanteys, sea 4:4, 19
chantwells 3:40
charanga 3:10
charango 3:25, 9:17
Charles, Ray 5:17, 6:47, 48
Charleston 5:45, 46
charts, hit-parade 8:37, 10:48
Chat Noir (Paris) 7:20, 21–22
Chavis, Boozoo 4:66
Checker Board Lounge 5:31
Chenier, C.J. 4:66
Chenier, Clifton 4:66
Cher 10:66–67
Chess label 5:32–33, 6:8, 8:47, 48
Chevalier, Maurice 7:15, 22
Chic 6:55
Chicago 5:27, 31, 34–36, 46–47, 48–49, 6:5
chicha 3:26
Chick Webb Orchestra 3:13
Chiffons 8:31
Child, James 4:23
Chile 3:30

China 1:6–8, 3:51–52, 9:5
Choates, Harry 4:67
choirs 10:38–45
church 1:23, 24, 10:40–43
Chopin, Frédéric 2:10–11, 12, 25
chorale preludes 1:47
chorales 1:45
choral singing 10:38–45
chords 1:22, 2:31
choro 3:27
chorus 1:24–25, 10:39
Chorus Line, A (Hamlisch) 7:43
chouval bwa 3:35
Christian, Charlie 5:53, 9:40, 41
Christian Church 1:7, 13–14, 8:6–7, 10:11–16, 39–43
Baroque cantatas 1:45
and negro spirituals 5:10–11
and the Renaissance 1:23–24
Christy Minstrels 5:8
chromatic scale 2:16, 17, 36
church music *See* Christian Church
Civil War, American 4:13–15, 16, 17
Clapton, Eric 5:27, 36, 38–39, 6:31, 65
clarinet 1:41, 9:21, 22–23
Clark, Dick 6:20
Clarke, Herbert L. 8:11
Clash 6:40–41
clausulas 1:15, 16
claves and clave rhythm 3:5, 6–7, 8
clavichord 1:53
Clayton, Buck 5:51, 52
Clegg, Johnny 3:67
Cleveland, James 5:17
Cliff, Jimmy 3:37, 38
Cline, Patsy 4:50, 51, 59
Clinton, George 6:54
Cobain, Kurt 6:45
Cochrane, Eddie 6:14
Coe, David Allen 4:57
Cohan, George M. 7:29–30
Cohen, Leonard 4:33, 34–35
Coleman, Cy 7:42
Coleman, Ornette 5:63, 64, 66
Cole, Nat "King" 5:54, 55
colleges *See* universities and colleges
Collins, Judy 4:33, 35
Colombia, and salsa 3:18–19
Colón, Willie 3:14, 15, 16
color, and music 2:27–28
Coltrane, John 5:61, 63, 66, 9:24
columbia rhythm 3:8
Combs, Sean "Puffy" 6:63
Commodores 6:56, 57
Como, Perry 10:52
compact disks (CDs) 6:43, 64, 8:65, 9:56, 67
making 8:66–67
recordable 9:66
compas 3:35
computers, recording on 8:61, 64, 9:64
concept albums 6:33
concert bands 8:11, 12
concert halls, American 4:16
concerto delle dame 10:15
concerto grosso 1:41
concerts
Baroque 1:42
first in America 4:6–7
concrete music 2:56–57
conductors 1:23–24, 2:12, 8:17–19
20th-century 2:54–55
conga (drum) 3:33, 5:57
conjunto 3:21, 4:53
Connick, Harry, Jr. 10:55
Conniff, Ray 7:65
conservatories, music 8:12–13
consoles, mixing 8:61–62, 63, 64–65
consonance 1:21, 2:31
continuo 1:34
contracts 8:30
contradanza 3:6, 9

contraltos 10:7–8, 37
conventions, musical 1:32
Cooder, Ry 3:18, 38, 59, 9:63
Cooke, Sam 5:17, 6:47
Cooper, Alice 6:37
copla 3:31
Copland, Aaron 2:52–53
copyright 7:21, 8:31, 51
cor anglais 9:21–22
Corea, Chick 5:63, 65–66
Corelli, Arcangelo 1:37
Corelli, Franco 10:36–37
Cornershop 3:47
cornett 1:40
counterpoint 2:28, 5:60, 62
countertenors 10:37
country music 4:36–61
Cuba's 3:9
Puerto Rico's 3:11
Couperin, François 1:43, 44, 2:64
Covay, Don 6:48
cowbell 3:12–13, 27
cowboys, songs 4:21–22
Cox, Ida 5:26, 29
Cray, Robert 5:39
Cream 5:38, 6:31
Creedence Clearwater Revival 5:39
Creoles 4:63, 5:43, 44
Crew Cuts 6:6
Cristofori, Bartolomeo 2:11, 9:37
crooning 5:55, 10:51
Crosby, Bing 4:45, 5:54, 55, 7:61, 10:9, 46, 50–51
Crosby, Stills, and Nash 4:33
cross-rhythms, and salsa 3:7
Crow, Sheryl 4:60
Crumb, George 10:64, 65
Cruz, Celia 3:14, 15
cuatro 3:6, 11, 9:17
Cuba/Cubans, and salsa 3:4–10, 12–18, 33
cuica 3:27
cumbia 3:23
cymbals 9:34
Cyrus, Billy Ray 4:61
Czechoslovakia, nationalist composers 2:23–25, 42–43, 10:45

D

da capo form 1:34
Dallapiccola, Luigi 10:19
dambura 3:49
Damned 6:41
Damrosch, Walter 4:16
Daniels, Charlie 4:58
danza 3:9
danzón 3:9–10
darabuka 3:56
Darbone, Luderin 4:64
dastgahs 3:57
DAT recording 9:53, 64, 65–66
David, Hal 5:19, 7:42, 10:55
Davidson, Eduardo 3:14
Davis, Miles 5:56, 59, 60, 62–63, 65, 66
DCC digital cassettes 9:66
death trail 7:14
Debussy, Claude 2:28, 30–32, 33, 40, 45, 5:6, 10:33
Decca label 5:30, 32
décimas 3:11, 23
Deep Purple 6:33, 35, 36
De Forrest, Lee 9:43
De Koven, Reginald 7:8–9
De La Rosa, Tony 3:22
De La Soul 6:61
delay 8:63–64, 10:66
Deller, Alfred 10:37

Delmore Brothers **4**:42, *43*
Delta blues **5**:23–24
Demonios de Mantaro, Los **3**:26
demo recordings **8**:45, 57–58
Denner, Christoph **9**:22
Depeche Mode **9**:*51*
dervishes **3**:*57*
Desmond, Paul **5**:*60*, 62
des Prés, Josquin **1**:*29*
development, of music **1**:*6–7*
devil **5**:28, 38
dhol **3**:49
dholak **3**:*47*
Diabate, Tourmani **3**:*60*
Diaghilev, Sergei **2**:39–40
Diamond, Neil **6**:24
Dickinson, John **4**:9
Diddley, Bo **6**:*9*
didgeridoo **9**:*29*
Dietrich, Marlene **7**:*24*, 25
digital recording **8**:*61*, **9**:*62*, 63–64
digital sampling **8**:23, 32, **9**:49
digital synthesizers **9**:49
Din, Hamza el- **3**:*56*
Dion, Celine **6**:65–66
directors, video **8**:*38*
Dire Straits **6**:*43*
disco **5**:19, **6**:55–57
discords **1**:*63*, **2**:16, 36
disk jockeys (DJs) **8**:*27*, 36, 40, **9**:*56*
   and hip-hop **6**:58–59
Disney, Walt *See* Walt Disney
dissonance **1**:30, **2**:24, 31, 38, 50
distortion **6**:32
distribution, music **8**:40–41
Dixie Chicks **4**:59
Dixie Hummingbirds **5**:16, 17
Dixie Ramblers **4**:64
Dixon, Willie **5**:35, 37, 38
D'León, Oscar **3**:19
dobro **4**:41
doctrine of the affections **1**:*32*, 33
Dolmetsch, Arnold **2**:*65–66*
Dolphy, Eric **5**:*64*, 67
Domingo, Placido **10**:*8*, 9, 28
Dominican Republic **3**:33
Domino, Fats **6**:*6*, 7, 8–9
Dominquez, Reutilio **3**:*9*
Donizetti, G. **10**:26
Donzelli, Domenico **10**:28–30
Doors **6**:*29–30*
doo-wop **5**:18, **6**:6, 18, **10**:59
Dorsey, Jimmy **5**:54
Dorsey, Thomas A. **5**:*14*, 31
Dorsey, Tommy **5**:54
doshpuluurs **3**:*53*
double bass **8**:*43*, **9**:6, 10–*11*
Doucet, Michael **4**:*67*
Douglas, Roy **2**:*46*
Dowland, John **1**:27
D'Oyly Carte, Richard **7**:*9*
Dr. Dre **6**:63
drill chants **5**:*7*
drum machines **9**:*52*
drums **1**:12, 19, **9**:*32*, 33–34
   Indian **3**:*45*, 46
   jazz **5**:*61*
   Native American **4**:*6*
   and salsa **3**:*7*
   steel **3**:*40*
dub **3**:*38*
Dufay, Guillaume **1**:*24*, 29
Duhon, Edwin **4**:*64*
Duke Ellington Orchestra **5**:*52*, **7**:*25*
dulcimer **4**:*39*
Duncan, Tommy **4**:*48*
Durante, Jimmy **7**:*15*
Durey, Louis **2**:44, *45*
dutar **3**:*49*
DVDs **9**:66, *67*
Dvořák, Antonín **2**:23–25, **5**:*11*
Dylan, Bob **4**:29–*31*, 32, **6**:25, 65
dynamics **1**:*30*, 32
dynamophone **9**:*43*

E

Earle, Steve **4**:*61*
early-music revival **2**:62–67
Earp, Wyatt **4**:22, *23*
easy-listening **7**:64, 65
Ebb, Fred **7**:42
Edison, Thomas A. **9**:54–55
education, music **8**:*4*, *7–13*
   See also teaching music
Edwards, Bernard **6**:55
Egypt **3**:55–56
   ancient **1**:5–6, *7*, **9**:*13*, 25, **10**:*10*
eisteddfods **1**:18
electronic music **2**:55–56, **10**:64–65
   film scores **7**:57
   instruments **9**:*42–53*
electronics, in pop vocals **10**:66–67
Elektra label **8**:48
Elfman, Danny **7**:60
Elgar, Edward **2**:46
Ellington, E.K. "Duke" **3**:13, **5**:15,
   50, 51, 52, 66
Emerson, Lake and Palmer **6**:33
EMI label **8**:*50*
Emmett, Dan **4**:13
engineers, sound **8**:*54–55*
enka **3**:*53*
Ephrata Cloisters **4**:7
Epstein, Brian **8**:*33–34*
Erato **1**:*9*
Este, Alfonso II d' **10**:*14*
Estefan, Gloria **3**:*16*, 17
Este, Isabella d' **10**:*14*
Ethiopia **3**:*57*
euphonium **9**:*31*
Europe, and jazz **5**:49–50
eurythmics **8**:*9*
Evans, Bill **5**:55, 63
Evans, Gil **5**:*60*
Everly Brothers **4**:*44*, **6**:15
Evers, Medgar **5**:65
Evora, Cesaria **3**:*61*
Experimental Band **5**:*64*
Expressionists **2**:35, 36, 52

F

Faddis, Jon **5**:*66*
fado **3**:26–27, 61
Failde, Miguel **3**:*9*
Fairlight CMI **8**:32
Faith, Percy **7**:65–*66*
Falcon, Joe **4**:*63*
Falla, Manuel de **2**:48
Fallen Angels **4**:*60*
falsetto **10**:13, 15, *59*
Farinelli **1**:*38*, **10**:16, *24*
Farm Aid **4**:57
Farmer, Art **5**:*40*
fasil **3**:*57*
Fauré, Gabriel **2**:28
feedback **6**:32
fees, artists' **8**:42
Fender, Freddy **4**:*53*
Fender, Leo **9**:40–*41*, 46, *47*
Ferrer, Ibrahim **3**:18
festivals, music **1**:18
fiddles/fiddle music **4**:39, *63*, **5**:*5*, 7
   and American settlers **4**:8, *12*, 13,
   20
fife-and-drum bands **4**:9, **5**:*5*
Finland, nationalist composers **2**:48–49
First Edition **4**:57
First New England School **4**:9
Fischer-Dieskau, Dietrich **10**:*9*
Fitzgerald, Ella **3**:13, **5**:56, **10**:50, *51*
Five Blind Boys **5**:*16*, 17
"Five, The" **2**:26–27
flamenco **2**:29, **3**:55
Flatt, Lester **4**:42, *43*
Fledermaus, Die (Strauss) **7**:*8*
Fleetwood Mac **5**:36, 39
floor-show bands **8**:22

flugelhorn **5**:*60*
flute **1**:*4*, 4:6, **9**:*20*–21
Flying Burrito Brothers **4**:60
Foley, Red **4**:41, 56
folk music **2**:24–27, 29, 42, 43–44,
   10:*19*
   Cuban *See son*
   United States **4**:18–35
   See also nationalist composers
folk pop **6**:25
foreground music **7**:*67*
forro **3**:*29*
Forrest, Helen **5**:*56*
Foster, Stephen **4**:*14*, **5**:*8*, 9
Foula **3**:35
4:40 **3**:*34*
Four Horsemen **5**:38
Four Tops **6**:20, *50*, 51
France **3**:6, **7**:22–24
   nationalist composers **2**:28–29,
   44–46
Franck, César **2**:28
Franco-Flemish school **1**:*29–30*, 31
Franklin, Aretha **6**:47, *48*
Franklin, Benjamin **4**:*7*, 8
Franklin, Kirk **5**:19
Freed, Alan **6**:*4*, *5–6*, 8, 14, **8**:36
free funk **5**:65
French Antilles **3**:35
French horn **9**:*29*
frequency **1**:*10*
Fresh Prince **6**:63
Fricke, Jane **4**:59
Friml, Rudolph **7**:*9–10*
Frizzell, "Lefty" **4**:40, 46–47
frontier, American **4**:11–12, 21–22
frottola **1**:25
fugues **1**:*47*, 66, **4**:*9*
function bands **8**:22
funk **5**:19, **6**:*51*, 52–55
Funkadelic **6**:54–55
fusion **5**:65–*66*, 67
Futurists **9**:*44*
fuzzboxes **6**:32

G

Gabrieli, Andrea **1**:*26*, 30
Gabrieli, Giovanni **1**:*30*–31
Galilei, Vincenzo **10**:*17*
gamelans **3**:*50*–51, **9**:*34*
gangsta rap **6**:61–63
garage (1990s) **6**:65
garage bands (1960s) **6**:23
Garcia, Jerry **6**:*28*
Gardiner, John Eliot **2**:*67*
Garfunkel, Art **4**:32, *33*
Garland, Judy **7**:18, *38*
Gaye, Marvin **6**:49–*50*
Gayle, Crystal **4**:59
Gaynor, Gloria **6**:55–56
gayup **3**:*40*
Genesis **6**:33
Gentry, Bobbie **4**:55
Germany, cabaret **7**:24–26
Gershwin, George **2**:*53*, **5**:*7*, **7**:*19*, 20,
   32–33, 35, **10**:*34*, 35–36
Gershwin, Ira **7**:*32*–33, 35
Gesualdo, Carlo **1**:*29*, *30*
Getz, Stan **3**:28, **5**:54, 62
ghazal **3**:*46*, 47, **9**:*29*
ghichak **3**:49
Gilberto, Joao and Astrud **3**:28–*29*
Gilbert and Sullivan **7**:*9*
Gilded Age, music of the **4**:16–17
Gil, Gilberto **3**:*29*
Gillespie, J.B. "Dizzy" **3**:13, **5**:*57*,
   58–59, 60, 66
Gill, Vince **4**:60
gittern **9**:*14*
Glass, Philip **2**:*60*, 61, **7**:59–60, **10**:*35*
Glinka, Mikhail **2**:25–26
glockenspiel **9**:35
Gluck, Christoph Willibald **1**:*61*

gods, music from the **1**:*7*
Goethe, J.W. **7**:*6*, **10**:*18*
Goffin, Gerry **6**:*16*, *17*, **8**:30
Golden Gate Quartet **5**:15, 17
Gold, Nick **3**:18
gold rush, Californian **4**:*21*, 39
goliards **1**:17–18, **10**:*12*
González, Celina **3**:*9*
González, Rubén **3**:18
Goodman, Benny **2**:64, **5**:47, *53–54*
goombay **3**:39
Gordy, Berry **5**:18, **6**:19, 49, 52, 53
gospel music **3**:67, **5**:*10*, 13–19
Gottschalk, L.M. **4**:10–11, **5**:*6*
Gounod, Charles **2**:28
Gow, Neil **4**:*12*
grace notes **2**:*9*
graffiti **6**:*58*
gramophones **8**:*46*, 47, **9**:55, *56*,
   10:*49*
Gran Combo, El **3**:18
Grand Funk Railroad **6**:36
Grandmaster Flash, DJ **6**:58, *59*, 60
Grand Ole Opry, The **4**:*41*
Granz, Norman **5**:56, 58
Grappelli, Stephane **5**:*49*
Grateful Dead **3**:39, **4**:*67*, **6**:*28*, **8**:*41*
Graun, Carl Heinrich **1**:52
Grease (Jacobs and Casey) **7**:*44*
Great Awakenings **4**:12, **5**:11
Great Britain, nationalist composers
   2:46–48
Great Depression **4**:*24*
Greece, ancient **1**:6, *7*, 7–8–11, 28,
   8:*4*–6, **9**:*5*, **10**:11, 38–*39*
Green, Al **5**:*16*, 17, **6**:47
Greenwich Village **4**:*28*
Gregorian chant
   See plainsong/plainchant
Gregory I, Pope **1**:*14*, **10**:*40*
Grenada **3**:33
Grieg, Edvard **2**:29
Griffith, Nancy **4**:34
Grillo, Frank *See* Machito
griots **3**:*58*, 60, **5**:20
Grisman, David **5**:*67*
Grossman, Albert **4**:27
ground bass **1**:*36*
grunge **6**:45, 66, **8**:*50*
Grupo Mackandal **3**:34
Guadeloupe **3**:35
guagua **3**:*5*
guaguacanó rhythm **3**:*8*
Guard, Dave **4**:25, 26
Guerra, Juan Luis **3**:34
Guido d'Arezzo **1**:*16*, 23, **10**:*40–41*
Guilbert, Yvette **7**:22–23, *24*
güiro **3**:*5*, 7, 33
guitar **4**:13, **5**:6, **9**:*14–18*, 35
   electric **6**:*32*, **9**:11, 17, *40–41*
   lap steel **5**:25, **9**:*40*
   one-string **5**:*5*
   salsa **3**:6, 11
   slide **3**:*62–63*, **5**:22, 23, *25*, 36
   tres **3**:6, 8, 9
guitarilla **9**:*17*
guitar synthesizers **5**:*67*
guitarrón **3**:*21*, **9**:*17*
Guns N' Roses **5**:38, **6**:36
Guthrie, Arlo **4**:25
Guthrie, W.W. "Woody" **4**:23–*24*, 25,
   26, 30
Guy, Buddy **5**:*31*, 36, *37*
Guy Lombardo and His Royal
   Canadians **5**:53
Guys and Dolls (Loesser) **7**:*40*
gwo ka **3**:35

H

Hackberry Ramblers **4**:*64*
Haggard, Merle **4**:46–47, 54–55
Hair (MacDermot) **7**:*47*
Haiti **3**:33, 34–35

Haley, Bill 6:5, 6, 10
Hamburg Opera House 1:*36*
Hamlisch, Marvin 7:43
Hammerstein, Oscar, II 7:11, 20, 31, 32
    Rodgers and 7:36–37, 41
Hammond, John 5:15, 53
Hampson, Thomas 10:9
Hancock, Herbie 5:*63*, 65
Handel, George F. 1:*37–40*, 10:16, *20, 23*
    Messiah 1:*33*, 10:43
    music revival 2:63
Handy, William Christopher 5:*22*, 30, 52
Harburg, "Yip" 7:38
hard bop 5:62
hardcore 6:43
Harlem 5:*44*, 45, 52
harmonica 5:*35*
    glass 4:*7*, 8
harmony 1:20, 21–22, 30, 44, 2:31
harp 1:19, 3:25, 30, 9:11–*13*
harpsichord 1:51, 56, 57, 2:11, *62*, 4:*7*, 9:*35*, 37
Harris, Charles K. 7:18–19, 10:48
Harris, Emmylou 4:60
Harrison, George 3:44, 45, 6:*22*, 27, 8:31
Harry, Debbie 6:41, *42*
Hart, Lorenz 7:33–34, 35, 36
Harumi, Miyako 3:53
hatzotzerah 1:12
Hawkins, Coleman 5:49, 51, 9:*24*
Hawkins, Edwin 5:17
Hawkins, Hawkshaw 4:51
Hawkins, Screamin' Jay 5:*28*
Haydn, Joseph 1:51, 53, *54–57*, 9:12, 27, 10:43
    and Beethoven 1:*63*, 64
    and Mozart 1:*60*
Hayes, Isaac 6:49, *51*, 7:62
Hayes, Lee 4:24
Headhunters 5:65
heavy metal 5:*38*, 6:34–37
Heinrich, Anthony Philip 4:10
Helmholtz, Hermann von 9:43
Henderson, Fletcher 5:*45–46*
Henderson, Joe 5:63
Hendrix, Jimi 5:*36*, 39, 6:10, 31–*32*, 33, 9:*41*
Herbert, Victor 7:9, *10*, 21, 29, *30*, 53
Herc Kool, DJ 6:59
Herman, Jerry 7:42
Herman, Woody 5:54
Herrmann, Bernard 7:56, 57
Heuberger, Richard 7:7
Hibari, Misora 3:53
hi-fi systems 9:57
"highlife" 3:59
Hillbillies 4:37, *38*
hillbilly music 4:37, 5:*7*, 6:10
Hiller, Johann Adam 7:6
Hill, Lauryn 6:63, *64*, 65, 67
Hillman, Chris 4:60
Hindemith, Paul 2:64–65, 9:*45–46*
Hines, Earl "Fatha" 5:48
Hinojosa, Tish 4:53
hip-hop 5:19, 6:45, 57, *58–63*, 7:63
hippy counterculture 6:27
hocket 3:30
hoedowns 4:20, 39
Hogwood, Christoper 2:67
Holiday, Billie 5:52, 54, *55*, 56
Holland-Dozier-Holland 6:20–21
hollers 5:22, *23*
    field 5:6, 7
Holly, Buddy 6:7, 12–*13*, 14, *15*, 9:61, 10:54
Hollywood 7:20
home entertainment 7:18
homophonic music 1:31, 52
Honegger, Arthur 2:44, 45–46, 7:52–53

honky-tonk 4:45–46, 55, 65
Hooker, John Lee 5:*32*, 37
hootenannies 4:26
"Hootenanny" 4:26, 28
Hopkinson, Francis 4:10
Hopkinson, Joseph 4:10
horn 9:28–30
Horne, Marilyn 10:7
Horton, Vaughan 4:45
Hot Five 5:46
Hot Seven 5:46
Houdini, Harry 7:*15*
house music 6:45, 65
House, Son 5:23–*24*, 26–27, 28
Houston, Cissy 5:*19*
Houston, Whitney 5:*19*, 6:65
Howe, Julia Ward 4:14
Howlin' Wolf 5:34, 35, 37, 6:32
huapango 3:22–23
huasteco 3:22–23
huayno 3:25
Humperdinck, Engelbert 10:63, *64*
Hungary, nationalist composers 2:25, 43–44, 10:45
Hüsker Dü 6:43
Hussain, Zakir 3:44–45
Huun-Huur-Tu 3:53
hydraulos/hydraulis 1:28, 9:35–36
hymns 1:13, 24, 4:4
    and slaves 5:11–12

I

Ice Cube 6:63
Impressionists 2:30–33
improvisation 1:58, 3:44
    modal 5:62–63
incantation 1:13
Incas 3:*23*, 30
incidental music 7:52, 67
India 1:7, 3:*42–46*
Indianapolis 5:31
Indonesia 2:32, 33, 3:50–51
Ink Spots 5:18
instrumental music 1:40
instrumentals, popular 7:65–66
instruments 9:4–41
    amplified 9:39–40
    authentic 2:65–66
    electronic 9:42–53
    first 1:4–5, 9:05
interludes 1:52
intermedi 1:*33*, 10:20–21, *42*
International Submarine Band 4:60
Internet 6:65, 8:39, 41, *51*
intervals 1:21
Inti Illimani 3:30
inventionshorn 9:30
Irakere 3:16
Iron Butterfly 6:35
iscathamiya 3:67, 10:62
Islamic world 3:*54–57*
Isley Brothers 6:51
Ito, Takio 3:52–53
Ives, Charles 2:34–35, 59

J

Jackson Five 6:51–52
Jackson, Janet 6:67
Jackson, Mahalia 5:15, 16, 17
Jackson, Michael 6:10, 51–52
Jacques-Dalcroze, Emile 8:8, *9*
Jagger, Mick 6:48
Jamaica 3:33, *36–37*
James Bond films 7:*61*, 62
James, Elmore 5:36
Jamestown 4:5
Jan and Dean 6:23–24
Janáček, Leoš 2:42–43, 10:45
Janequin, Clément 10:13
Jane's Addiction 6:45
Japan 3:*52–53*

Jara, Victor 3:*30*
Java 3:50
Jayhawks 4:61
jazz 5:*40–67*
    Afro-Cuban 3:13, 5:57
    big-band 5:50–54
    Blue Note label 5:64, 8:47, 48, 49
    blues scale 5:21
    careers in 8:20–21
    Chicago-style 5:46–47
    cool 5:59–62
    free 5:63–64
    jazz-rock fusion 5:65–66
    Latin-American 3:13–14, 5:57
    modal 5:62–63
    modern 5:59
    New Orleans/traditional 5:42–44, 46, 50, 66
    "polite" 5:45
    ragtime 5:9, 41
    and scat singing 5:46, 55
    township 3:67
    See also bebop; boogie-woogie; hard bop; swing
jazz age 5:45
Jazz Hounds 5:25
Jazz Messengers 5:62, 67, 8:21
jazz-rock fusion 5:65–66
Jazz Singer, The 7:*17*, 35, *60–61*
Jazz Workshop 5:64
Jefferson Airplane 6:28–29
Jefferson, Blind Lemon 5:28, 30–31, 8:*47*
Jennings, Waylon 4:57, 6:15
Jesus Christ Superstar (Lloyd Webber) 7:45–46
jibaro 3:15, 18
Jimenez, Don Santiago 3:21–22
Jimenez, Flaco 3:21–22, 4:53
Jimmy James and the Blue Flames 6:32
jingles 7:64, 66–*67*, 8:23
Jobim, Antonio Carlos 3:28–29
John, Elton 7:49
Johnson, Freddy 5:49
Johnson, James P. 5:*47–48*, 64
Johnson, Lonnie 5:28, 31, 32
Johnson, Pete 5:32, 49
Johnson, Robert 5:24, 26–*27*, 28, 38
joik singing 10:59–60
Jolson, Al 7:*17*, 32, 60–61
Jones, Elvin 5:*61*
Jones, George 4:*46*, 47
Jones, Philly Joe 5:61
Jones, Quincy 8:55
jongleurs 1:*17*, 10:12
Joplin, Janis 6:29
Joplin, Scott 5:*41*, 43, 10:49
Josquin des Prés 1:*29*
juarana 9:17
jubilee quartet singing 5:17
Jubilee Singers 5:*12–13*, 17
jubilees (spirituals) 5:11
Judd, Naomi and Wynonna 4:59
jug bands 5:30
juju 3:59–60
Jungle Brothers 6:61

K

Kaempfert, Burt 7:65, 66
kalindula 3:64–65
Kander, John 7:42
Kandinsky, Wassily 2:35
Kansas City, and the blues 5:32
Kante, Mory 3:58–59
karnatak 3:45–46
Karajan, Herbert von 2:*55*, 8:18
Kassav 4:51
Kassau 3:36
kayokyoku 3:53
kazoo 5:30
kecak 3:51
Keiser, Reinhard 1:37
Keith-Albee circuit 7:14

Kelly, Gene 7:38
Kelly, R. 6:*67*
kena 3:24
Kenton, Stan 5:57, 60
Keppard, Freddie 5:43–44
keras 1:9
Kern, Jerome 7:11, 31–32, 35, 36, 37
Kershaw, Doug 4:66–*67*
keyboard instruments 1:*22*, 9:6, 35–39
    sampling keyboards 8:32
Key, Francis Scott 4:*11*
Khaled, Cheb 3:55, *56*
Khan, Ali Akbar 3:*42*, 43–44
Khan, Baba Allauddin 3:43
Khan, Nusrat Fateh Ali 3:*48*
Khan, Rahat Fateh Ali 3:48
Khusrau, Amir 3:43
Kidjo, Angélique 3:60
King, B.B. 5:*33–34*
King, Carole 4:35, 6:*16, 17*, 24, 8:30
King Cole Trio 5:55
King Crimson 6:33
King, Freddie 5:36
King, Martin Luther, Jr. 4:28, *29*, 5:15, 16, 6:26
King Oliver's Creole Jazz Band 5:*43*, 44
King, Pee Wee 4:45
King Records 5:33
Kingsmen 6:23
Kingston Trio 4:25–26, *27*, 28, 34
King Tubby 3:38
kinnor 1:12
Kirkpatrick, Ralph 2:66
Kirshner, Don 6:*17*
kithara 1:*9*, 11
klarnet 3:57
Kleban, Edward 7:43
Kodály, Zoltán 2:43–44, 8:*10*, 10:19, 45
kora 3:59, *60*
Korn 6:67
Korngold, Erich 7:55
koto 3:52
Kraftwerk 9:*50–51*, 10:66
Kristofferson, Kris 4:57
Krupa, Gene 5:47, 53, 61
Ktesibios 1:28, 9:37
Kussudiardja, Bagong 3:51
Kuti, Fela 3:*62*
kwela 3:64, 66

L

labels, as companies 8:46–47
La Bohème (Puccini) 2:18
Ladysmith Black Mambazo 3:67, 10:*62*, 63
La India 3:17
Laine, Cleo 10:6
la-la music 4:66
lambada 3:29, 36
lamentations 1:29
Landini, Francesco 1:25
lang, k.d. 4:59
Lanner, Joseph 2:15
laoud 3:9
Lapland 10:59–60
Larson, Jonathan 7:48
Lasso, Orlando di 1:26, 29–30, *31*
Latin American music 3:23–31
    See also Mexico; salsa
La Traviata (Verdi) 2:18, 10:29
Lauder, Sir Harry 7:15
Lavoe, Héctor 3:15
"Leadbelly" 4:23, *25*, 5:28, 29, 38
Led Zeppelin 5:*38*, 6:*34*, 36
Lee, Brenda 4:59
Lee, Johnny 4:58
Lee, Peggy 5:56, 10:*51–52*
Lehár, Franz 7:7, 8
Lehman, Lotte 10:34
Leiber, Jerry 8:*30*

leitmotifs **2**:16
Lejeune, Iry **4**:*64*, 65
Lemper, Ute **7**:*27*
Lennon, John **6**:*22, 27*, **8**:*33, 56*
Léonin **1**:15
Lerner and Loewe **7**:39
*Les Misérable*s (Schönberg) **7**:47–48
Lesser Antilles **3**:33
Lewis, George **5**:66
Lewis, Jerry Lee **6**:*4*, 7, 12, 14
Lewis, John **5**:60, 66
Lewis, Meade "Lux" **5**:*49*, **8**:49
Lewis, Willie **5**:49
lieder **2**:7, 14, **10**:18, 27
Light Crust Doughboys **4**:48
light music **7**:64, 65
Limp Bizkit **6**:67
line-dancing **4**:61
Lion, Alfred **8**:*49*
Lion King, The **7**:49
lira da braccio **9**:6
Liszt, Franz **2**:9, *10*, 25, **9**:*36*
Little Eva **6**:*16*, 17
Little Richard **6**:7, *9–10*, 14, **10**:67
Little Walter **5**:35
Lloyd Webber, Andrew **7**:*45–47*
Lobos, Los **3**:*22*
Locatelli, Pietro Antonio **1**:43
Locke, Matthew **1**:35–36
Loewe, Frederick **7**:39
Lomax, Alan **3**:39, **4**:22, 23, **5**:43
Lomax, John A. **4**:23
Lombardo, Guy **5**:53
London, and rock **6**:30–31
long-playing albums (LPs) **8**:37
loops **8**:32
Lopez brothers **3**:12
Los Angeles, and the blues **5**:32
lounge music **7**:65
Louvin Brothers **4**:42–43
Lovett, Lyle **4**:60
Lovin' Spoonful **6**:25
Lukather, Steve **8**:*23*
Lully, Jean-Baptiste **1**:*35*
lute **1**:*18*, 22, 26–28, **4**:*7*, **9**:14, **10**:*15*
Luther, Martin **1**:24
Lymon, Frankie **6**:*6*
Lynn, Loretta **4**:50, *51–52*
lyre **1**:*9*, 11, **10**:*11*

M

Maal, Baaba **3**:58–59
McCartney, Paul **6**:*22, 27*, **8**:*56*
McCorkle, Susannah **7**:*27*
MacDowell, Edward **4**:16–17
McEntire, Reba **4**:59
McGee, Alan **8**:*45*
McGee, Dennis **4**:*64*, 67
McGhee, Brownie **5**:32, 37
Machito **3**:13, **5**:57
McLachlan, Sarah **4**:34
McLaren, Malcolm **8**:*35*
McLaughlin, John **5**:65
McLean, Jackie **5**:65, *67*
Macon, Uncle Dave **4**:41
Madagascar **3**:63–64
Madonna **3**:19, **6**:66
madrigals **1**:25–26, **4**:*7*, **10**:14, *15*
Magic Flute, The (Mozart) **1**:61, 62, **7**:*6*
Magic Sam **5**:36
magnetophone **9**:61
Mahavishnu Orchestra **5**:65
mahfil **3**:44
Mahlathini and the Mahotella Queens **3**:*66*
Mahler, Gustav **2**:19–20, **10**:18–19, 44, *45*
Mamas and the Papas **6**:25
mambo **3**:12–13
managers **8**:33–36
Mancini, Henry **7**:61

mandolin, and country music **4**:39, *42*
Mandrell, Barbara **4**:58–59
Mangeshkar, Lata **3**:46
Manilow, Barry **10**:55
Mann, Barry **8**:30
Mannheim school **1**:*58*
Manson, Marilyn **6**:*67*
Mapfumo, Thomas **3**:*65*
marabi **3**:67
maracas **3**:5, *8, 10*
Marais, Marin **1**:*40*
Maravillas del Siglo, Las **3**:12
marching bands **4**:9, **8**:11, 12, *17*, **9**:24, *31*
Marcovicci, Andrea **7**:*27*
mariachi music **3**:*20*–21
marimbula **3**:8
marinera **3**:25
Marley, Bob **3**:*38*
marrabenta **3**:65
Marriage of Figaro, The (Mozart) **1**:61–62, **10**:*26*
Marsalis, Wynton **5**:*40*, 66, **8**:*13*
Martenot, Maurice **9**:45
Martha and the Vandellas **6**:20
Martin, Dean **10**:*46*, 53
Martinez, Narciso **4**:53
Martinez, Sabu **5**:57
Martin, George **8**:56
Martin Guerre (Boubil and Schönberg) **7**:48
Martinique **3**:35–36
Martin, Ricky **3**:*19*
Marvelettes **6**:20
Mason, Lowell **8**:*10*–11
masques **1**:35
Massive Attack **3**:48
Mattea, Kathy **4**:59
Maxwell Davies, Peter **10**:65–66
Mayall, John **5**:38
Mayerbeer, Giacomo **10**:32–33
Mayfield, Curtis **6**:51, **7**:63, **10**:*59*
Maynard, Ken **4**:44
mazhar **3**:56
mazurka **2**:25
mbaqanga **3**:66, **10**:62
mbube **10**:62
MCs **6**:59
MC Hammer **6**:63
media music **8**:23
Meisel, Edmund **7**:*52*
Melchior, Lauritz **10**:*34*
Mellotron **8**:32
melodeon **4**:13
melodies **1**:21, 32, 33
Melody Boys **4**:*51*
Memphis **5**:*20*, 30
Memphis Jug Band **5**:30
Memphis Minnie **5**:26
Memphis Slim **5**:35, 37
Menard, D.L. **4**:65–66
Mendelssohn, Felix **2**:*7*–8, 63, **10**:43, 44
Menken, Alan **7**:49
mento **3**:36
Menuhin, Sir Yehudi **8**:*15*
Mercer, Johnny **4**:45
merchandising **8**:*41*, 42
merengue **3**:16, 33–34
méringue **3**:33, 35
Merman, Ethel **7**:37, 42
Messiaen, Olivier **2**:*58*
Messiah (Handel) **10**:*43*
Metallica **6**:36–37
metallophones **3**:50
metered verses **4**:5
Metheny, Pat **5**:*66*, 67
Method Man **6**:63
Metro-Goldwyn-Mayer, musicals **7**:35, 38
Metropolitan Opera House **4**:17, **10**:*31*, 37
Mexico **3**:20–23
mezzo-sopranos **10**:6–8
Miami Sound Machine **3**:17
Mickey-Mousing **7**:52

Micrologus **1**:16
microphones **5**:54, 55, **9**:39, *57–58, 59*, **10**:*48*, 49
Middle Ages **1**:13, 17–19, 21, **9**:38–39, **10**:12–13, 20
MIDI technology **9**:51–53
Mighty Sparrow **3**:40–41
Milano, Canova da **1**:28
Miles, Arthur **4**:57
Milhaud, Darius **2**:44, 45, 46
military bands **8**:17, **9**:*28*
Miller, Glenn **5**:*53*, 54, **7**:61
Miller, Rice **5**:34–35
Millöcker, Carl **7**:7
Mills Brothers **5**:18
Mills, Kerry **7**:19
milónga **3**:31
minimalism **2**:60–61, **10**:*35*, 36
Ministry **6**:67
Minnelli, Liza **7**:24, 42–43
minidiscs **8**: 65, **9**:66
minimalism — [see above]
Minton's Playhouse **5**:*58*, 59
minuet and trio **1**:52, 55
min'yo **3**:52–53
minstrel shows/troupes **4**:*13*, 14, **5**:*7–9*, **10**:19
minstrels, wandering **1**:17–18, 19, 24, **10**:12, *13*
in America **4**:18–19, **5**:20
Mississippi Delta blues **5**:23–24
Mitchell, Joni **4**:33–34, *35*
mixdown **8**:62
mixing consoles **8**:61–62, 63, 64–65
modal improvisation **5**:62–63
Modern Jazz Quartet (MJQ) **5**:60
Modern label **5**:33
modern R&B **6**:63, 67
modes **1**:10, 14, 21
  Dorian **8**:5
  Phrygian **3**:6, **8**:5
  Yo **3**:53
modulations **1**:30, 52, **2**:6
monasteries/monks **1**:13, 14, 23, **10**: *41*
Mongolia **3**:53, **10**:*57*–58
Monkees **6**:24
Monk, Theolonius **5**:*58*, 59, 63, **8**:49, **9**:*24*
monody **1**:20–21, 33–34, **10**:17
monophonic music **1**:8, **9**:61
Monroe, Bill **4**:41–42
Monroe Brothers **4**:43
Montana, Vince **6**:55
Montand, Yves **7**:23
Monteverdi, Claudio **1**:34, **10**:14, 16, *21*, 22, 42
Moog, Robert **9**:48–49
Moors **3**:6, 55, **9**:14
moral influence, music as **8**:5–6
Moreschi, Alessandro **10**:16, *17*
Morissette, Alanis **4**:34, **6**:66
Morley, Thomas **1**:25, 26
Morocco **3**:55
Morricone, Ennio **7**:59
Morrison, Jim **6**:29–30
Morrissey, Steven **6**:44
Morton, Benny **5**:66
Morton, Jelly Roll **5**:*43*, 66
motets **1**:16–17, 18, 31
Motown label **6**:*19*–21, 49–52, 53, **8**:48
Moulin Rouge (Paris) **7**:*21*
mouth music **10**:63
movements, in the symphony **1**:52
movies **7**:50–63
  "blaxploitation" **6**:51
  "Bollywood" **3**:46, *47*
  playing music for **8**:23–24
  reggae **3**:37
  and rock 'n' roll **6**:10
  "singing cowboy" **4**:*44*
  surf **6**:*23*

See also musicals, Hollywood
Mozart, Wolfgang Amadeus **1**:51, 53, *57–62*, 63, **4**:8, **10**:25
  operas **1**:60–62, **7**:*6*, **10**:25, *26*
  and Tchaikovsky **2**:64
MP3 format **8**:51, 65, *67*
MPB (*musica popular brasiliera*) **3**:29
mridangam **3**:46
MTV (Music Television) **8**:38
Mudhoney **6**:45
muezzins **3**:*54*
muliza **3**:25
Mulligan, Gerry **5**:60, 62
Muñequitos de Matanzas, Los **3**:9
Muses (goddesses) **1**:*7*
musica campesina **3**:9
musica jibara **3**:11
Musical Brownies **4**:48
musicals **7**:28–49
  Broadway **7**:17, 18, 29–34, 36–40, 41–49
  Hollywood **7**:29, 35–36, 38, 40–41
musica reservata **1**:29
music business **8**:28–43
music-drama **2**:15–16, **10**:20–21
music hall shows *See* vaudeville
"music of the spheres" **1**:10
music therapy **8**:25
musique concrète **2**:56–57
Mussorgsky, Modest **2**:26–27, **9**:24
mutes **1**:42
muzak **7**:67
mazurka **2**:25
My Fair Lady (Lerner and Loewe) **7**:*39*
mystery plays **10**:20

N

nadasvaram **3**:46
Nascimento, Milton **3**:29
Nash, Graham **4**:33
Nashville Sound **4**:49–50
Nashville West **4**:54
nationalist composers **10**:45
  in the 1800s **2**:22–29
  in the 1900s **2**:42–53
Native Americans **4**:5, *6*, 62, *63*, 64
Naughty Marietta (Herbert) **7**:*30*
N'Dour, Youssou **3**:58–*59*
Neefe, Christian Gottlob **1**:63
Nelson, Willie **4**:*57*
Neoclassical music **2**:40–41
Nepal **3**:48–49
New Christy Minstrels **4**:57
Newman, Alfred **7**:53–55
Newman, Jimmy C. **4**:67
New Orleans **5**:41–44, **6**:8–9
New Orleans Rhythm Kings **5**:46–47
Newport Folk Festival **4**:30–31, *34, 35*
Newton, Juice **4**:58
new wave **6**:41–43, **8**:50
New York City **3**:35, **5**:44–45
  See also Cotton Club; Tin Pan Alley
nightclubs, American **7**:26
Nine Inch Nails **6**:45, 67
Nirvana **6**:45, 66–67
Nixon in China (Adams) **2**:*61*
Nordraakin, Rikard **2**:29
norteño music **3**:21, *22*
Norway, nationalist composers **2**:29
notation **1**:15, 16, *19*, **10**:40–41
  ancient Greek **8**:4
  tablature **1**:27
  See also printed music
notes **1**:10
  "bent" **5**:21, 22
Notorious B.I.G. **6**:63
nueva canción **3**:15, 18, 26, 30, 31
nueva trova **3**:18
nuevo ritmo **3**:12–13
nuevo tango **3**:31
NWA (Niggers With Attitude) **6**:62–63

O

Oasis 8:39, *45*
oboe 9:*21*
ocarina 1:8
Ochoa, Eliades 3:*18*
Ochs, Phil 4:28, 31
Ockeghem, Johannes 1:29
octaves, and Pythagoras 1:10
Offenbach, Jacques 7:6–7
Oklahoma! (Rodgers and
    Hammerstein) 7:*36*
Oliver! (Bart) 7:*28*
Oliver, J. "King" 5:*43*, 44, 47
ondes martenots 2:56, 58, 9:45
opera buffa 1:60–61, 7:4, 5
opera comique 7:5, 10:33–34
operas 1:21, 7:4, 10:21–37
    American 4:10, *11*
    ballad 7:5
    Baroque 1:32–38
    Chinese 3:*51*
    English 1:35–36, 2:47–48
    first 1:33–34, 10:*21–22*
    French 1:34–*35*, 10:32–34
    German 1:36–38, 10:27–28
    light/comic *See* operettas
    music-drama 2:15–16, 10:20–21
    rock 7:44–47, *48*
    Romantic era 2:5–6, 18
    "Savoy" 7:9
opera seria 1:60
opera singers 8:19, *20*, 10:6–9
    first recordings of 8:*46*, 47
operettas 7:4–11, 29, *30*
Oppenheimer, Joselino "Bumbún"
    3:12
oratorios 1:38–39, 10:43–44
Orbison, Roy 6:15
orchestras 1:*65*, 66, 2:5, *12*
    "original" performances 2:66–67
    playing in 8:15–16
    recording 8:*58*, 59
    for silent motion pictures 7:51–52
    theater pit 8:*24*
    in the U.S. 8:11
orchestration 1:30–31
orchestrions 9:42
Orfeo (Monteverdi) 10:*21*, 22
Orff, Carl 8:8, 10:*44*, 45
organ 1:*28*, 7:51, 9:6, 35–37, *38*–39
    Hammond 9:46
organistrum 1:19
organum 1:14–15, *21*, 10:41
Original Creole Band 5:44
Original Dixieland Jazz Band 5:44, 46
Orioles 5:18
ornaments, musical 1:32, *33*, 44
Ory, Edward "Kid" 5:44, 46
oscillators 9:43
Os Ingênuos 3:27
ostinatos 2:60
oud 3:55, 63, 9:*14*
"outlaw movement" 4:57
overdubbing 8:60–61, 9:61
overtones 2:60
overtures 1:35, 48, 52
Owens, Buck 4:54, *56*

P

Pablo, Augustus 3:38
pachanga 3:14
Pacheco, Johnny 3:14–15
paean 1:9
Paganini, Nicolò 2:*10*, 9:*9*
Page, Hot Lips 5:52
Page, Jimmy 5:*38*, 6:31
Page, Patti 4:45
pagode 3:27
Pakistan 3:46–48
Palace Theater 7:14–15, 16
Palestrina, Giovanni da 1:26,
    28–*29*, 10:*42*

pallilos 3:10
Palmieri, Eddie 3:13–14
"palm-wine" music 3:59
pandeiro 3:*27*
pandereta 3:11
panpipes 1:7, 9, 3:23–24, *25*
Paramount label 5:29, *31*
Paris 2:*30*, 32, 33, 7:*20*, *21*–22, 8:20
Parker, Charlie "Bird" 5:*56*, *57*–58,
    59, 60, 9:24
Parker, Colonel Tom 6:11, 8:*34*
Parliament 6:54–55
Parsons, Gram 4:*60*
partitas 1:48
Parton, Dolly 4:53–*54*
parts, and harmony 1:21, 22
Pastor, Antonio (Tony) 7:*13*, 10:47
Patton, Charley 5:23, 24, 26–27
Paul, Les 9:*61*
Pavarotti, Luciano 10:9, *28*
Pavitt, Bruce 8:*50*
Paycheck, Johnny 4:57
payola scandal 6:14, 8:*36*
Peace Jubilees 4:17
Pearl Jam 6:45
Pears, Peter 10:*19*, 36, 37
Peer, Ralph 4:37, *38*
Peers, Bill 4:51
pedal boards 1:28
Penguins 5:18
Pepper, Art 5:60–62
percussion 1:5, 9, 3:27, 9:31–35
    Native American 4:5, 6
    salsa 3:5, *7*, 8
Peri, Jacopo 1:34, 10:*17*, 21–22
Perkins, Carl 6:12
Pérotin 1:15
Perry, Lee "Scratch" 3:*37*
Persia 3:57
Pestalozzi, Johann Heinrich 8:*8*
Peter, Paul, and Mary 4:26–27
Peterson, Oscar 5:55, *58*
Peter and the Wolf (Prokofiev) 2:51,
    9:21, 23
Petrucci, Ottaviano dei 1:23
Petty, Norman 6:14, 9:61
phase shifting 2:61
Philadelphia International Records
    6:55
Phillips, Sam 6:5, 10, 11, 12
phonographs 2:*43*, 44, 4:37, 5:44,
    9:54–55, 10:49
Piaf, Edith 7:*23*
piano 1:*14*, 9:6, 35, 37–*38*
    electric 9:46–*47*
    "prepared" 2:58
piano music 9:36
    jazz 5:47–49
    for silent motion pictures 7:51
Piazzolla, Astor 3:31, 5:*67*
"pickers" 4:48
Pickett, Wilson 6:48
picks 1:9, 27, 9:*18*
Pierce, Webb 4:47
Pilgrims 4:*4*, 5–6
Pine, Courtney 5:*66*
Pine Grove Boys 4:65
Pink Floyd 6:*33*
pioneers, American 4:11–*12*, 19–20,
    21–22
pipa 1:8, 3:51, 52
pitch 1:33, 8:5, 9:6
pizzicato 1:42, 9:11
plagiarism 8:31
plainsong/plainchant (Gregorian
    chant) 1:13, *14*, 15, 8:6, 10:40–41
    and harmony 1:21
    and Holst 2:47
    and polyphonic works 1:31
plantation songs 5:6–7
Plant, Robert 5:*38*
Plato 1:8, 8:*5*
playlists 8:40
plectra 9:18
plena 3:*11*–12, 18

pluggers 7:19, 8:39–40
Poland, nationalist composers 2:25
polkas 4:63
polonaises 2:25
polyphony 1:15, 52, 10:41
polyrhythms, and salsa 3:7
Pop, Iggy 6:*39*
pop music 6:16–25
    careers in 8:21–22
    film scores 7:62–63
Porgy and Bess (Gershwin) 7:*33*, 10:*34*,
    35–36
Porpora, Niccola Antonio 1:54
portamento 2:66, 10:33
Porter, Cole 4:45, 7:*34*, 37–39
posters 8:39
Poulenc, Francis 2:44, 45
Poulsen, Valdemar 9:58–60
Powell, Earl "Bud" 5:59, 8:49
Pozo, Chano 3:13, 5:57
Prado, Perez Pantalon 3:*12*
Praetorius, Michael 1:45
preludes, Bach's 1:47
prerecorded sound 2:56–57
Presley, Elvis 5:18, 6:5, 7, 10–*11*, 14,
    7:66, 8:*34*, 10:48
    manager 6:11, 8:*34*
    record label 8:48
Price, Ray 4:47
Pride, Charley 4:*56*
Prince 6:10, *57*
Prince Igor (Borodin) 2:26
Príncipe 3:61, 62
printed music 1:23
prison farms 5:23
Procul Harum 6:33
producers, recording studio 8:55–57
production music 7:67
professional musicians 8:14, 17
program music 2:8, 9
Prokofiev, Sergei 2:49, 50–51, 9:21
promoters 8:42
protest songs 4:28
psalmody 4:5
psalms 1:13, 31
    of the Pilgrims and Puritans 4:4, 5,
    6
psalters 4:5
Public Enemy 6:60, 61
publishing industry, music 7:*18*–20,
    8:29, 30
Puccini, Giacomo 2:*18*, 10:*31*, 32
Puckett, Riley 4:38
Puente, Tito 3:13, 14, 5:57
Puerto Rico 3:4, 10–13, 18, 33
"Puff Daddy" 6:63, 67
punk rock 6:37–41, 8:35, 50
    See also new wave
Purcell, Henry 1:*36*, 9:27
Puritans 4:5, 6
puys 1:18
Pythagoras 1:*10*, 8:5

Q

qawwali 3:47–48
quadrilles 4:63
quartets 1:53
    barbershop 10:*44*
    string 9:*12*
Quintette du Hot Club de France 5:*49*

R

Raa Negra 3:28
race music 5:7, 8:47–48
race records 5:30, 46
Rachmaninov, Sergei 2:*21*
radio 10:*50*
    and country music 4:37, 41, 58
Rafi, Mohammed 3:46
ragas 3:43–44
ragga 3:38

ragtime 5:9, 41, 10:49
rai 3:55, *56*
railroads, American 4:22
Rainey, Gertrude "Ma" 5:14, 24, 29,
    46
Raitt, Bonnie 5:*25*, 39
Rameau, Jean-Philippe 1:43, *44*–45
Ramones 6:39, *40*
ranchera 3:*22*
Ranks, Shabba 3:38
rap 3:38, 5:19, 6:59–63, 67, 7:63,
    10:*67*
    gangsta rap 6:61–63
Rara Machine 3:34
rasp, Native American 4:6
Ravel, Maurice 2:*30*, 32–*33*, *34*, 64
Ravens 5:18
raves 6:65
Rayne-Bo Ramblers 4:64–65
Razumovsky, Count 1:*64*, 65
RCA label 8:48
rebab 3:49, 51, 56
recitative 1:34, 2:25, 10:17–18, 22
record companies 8:44–51
    independent and major 8:47–51
    and marketing 8:37–40
recorder (instrument) 9:20
recording
    history of 9:54–67, 10:49
    MIDI-based 9:51–53
    process 8:52–67
recording studios 8:52–53, 58–59, 62,
    9:*60*, 64
record players 9:55–56, *57*
records 8:*36*–37, 9:55, 56–57
    making 8:65–66, 9:55
Redding, Otis 6:47, 49
Red Hot Chili Peppers 6:43–44, 67
Red Hot Peppers 5:43
Redman, Don 5:50–*51*
Reed, Lou 3:15, 6:37–39
reels, Scottish 4:*12*, 63, 10:63
Reese, Della 5:*17*
Reeves, Jim 4:49–50
reggae 3:36, *37*–38
Reich, Steve 2:*60*, 61
Reinhardt, Django 5:*49*
R.E.M. 6:*44*–45, 8:51
remix producers 8:56–57
Renaissance 1:19, 20–31, 52
Rent (Larson) 7:*48*
Reparata and the Delrons 6:18
retailing, music 8:40–41
reverb 8:*62*, 63
revival, early music 2:62–67
Revolutionary War era 4:9–*10*, 5:5
revues 7:16, 30–31
Reynolds, Nick 4:25
Rhodes, Harold 9:46
rhythm
    and church music 1:14
    and conducting 1:24
    and the Greeks 1:10
rhythm and blues (R&B) 5:18, 32,
    6:4–5, 31
Rice, T.D. "Daddy" ("Jim Crow")
    4:13, 5:*7*
Rice, Tim 7:45, 46, 49
Richard, Zachary 4:67
Rich, Buddy 5:54, 61
Richie, Lionel 6:*56*, 57
Richter, Franz Xavier 1:58
riffs 5:42, 6:34, 10:*67*
Riley, Terry 2:60
Rimsky-Korsakov, Nikolai 2:*27*, 39
Ring of the Nibelung, The (Wagner)
    2:16, 10:33, *34*
ripieno 1:43
Rite of Spring, The (Stravinsky) 2:40,
    41, 44
ritornello 1:43
Ritter, Tex 4:44
Roach, Max 5:61, 64
road crew ("roadies") 8:43
Roberts, Marcus 5:66

Robeson, Paul **5**:*13*, **7**:31, **10**:*9*
Robinson, "Smokey" **6**:19, 20, **10**:59
rock **6**:26–45
  alternative **6**:43–45
  folk **4**:31
  glam **6**:37, **7**:49
  heavy *See* heavy metal
  industrial **6**:67
  jazz-rock fusion **5**:65–66
  progressive **6**:33–34
  psychedelic **6**:28–33
  punk **6**:37–41, **8**:35, 50
  rock opera **7**:44–47, 48
  soft **4**:35
  See also jazz-rock fusion; rock 'n'
    roll
"Rocket 88" (record) **6**:5, 32
Rockin' Dopsie **4**:66
Rockin' Sidney **4**:66
rock 'n' roll **6**:4–15, **7**:20, 44, **8**:48,
  10:52
rock steady **3**:37
Rodgers and Hammerstein **7**:36–37,
  41
Rodgers and Hart **7**:33–34, 35
Rodgers, Jimmie **4**:38, 39–40, 46,
  10:*58*
Rodgers, Nile **6**:55
Rodriguez, Johnny **4**:53
Rogers, Kenny **4**:57–58
Rogers, Shorty **5**:60–62
Rolling Stones **5**:36, 37–38, **6**:*21*, 23,
  9:*41*
Rollins, Sonny **5**:*62*, 65
Romani, Antonio **10**:*22*
Romantic era **1**:67, **2**:4–21, **8**:7
Romberg, Sigmund **7**:9, 10–*11*
Rome, ancient **1**:*6*, 11–12, **10**:*11*
Romeu, Antonio María **3**:10
rondador **3**:*24*
Ronettes **5**:18, **6**:19
Ronstadt, Linda **3**:22
Root, George Frederick **4**:15
Rose, Fred **4**:46, 49
Rose Marie (Friml) **7**:*10*
Rosenfeld, Monroe **7**:19
Ross, Diana **6**:20, 21
Rossini, G.A. **10**:26
Rotten, Johnny **6**:38
Rousseau, Jean-Jacques **8**:7–8
royalties **7**:21, **8**:30, 55
Rubini, Giovanni **10**:27
Rudder, David **3**:*41*
rumba **3**:4, 5–7, 17, 62
rumbira **3**:65
Run D.M.C. **6**:*60*
Rush, Otis **5**:34, 35, 36, 37
Russell, George **5**:66
Russia
  nationalist composers **2**:25–28
  See also Soviet Union
Russolo, Luigi **9**:*44*
Russo, William **5**:66
Rusty and Doug **4**:67

S

Sacred Harp, The **4**:12–13
Sahm, Doug **4**:53
Saint Domingue **3**:6
St. Matthew Passion (Bach) **1**:49, **2**:63
St. Prix, Dédé **3**:35
Salieri, Antonio **1**:62, 63
Salome (Strauss) **2**:20
Salomon, Johann Peter **1**:56–57
salpinx **1**:9
salsa **3**:4–*19*, **5**:57
samba **3**:27, 28
Sam and Dave **6**:49
Sami music **10**:59–*60*
Sammartini, Giuseppe **1**:60
sampling **8**:32, **9**:49, **10**:67
Santamaria, Mongo **5**:57

Santana **6**:65
sarangi **3**:48
sarinda **3**:49
sarod **3**:42, *43*
Satie, Erik **2**:44–*45*, **7**:21
Savuka **3**:*67*
Sao Tomé **3**:61, 62
saxophone **9**:19, 21, 23–24
scales
  blues **5**:21
  chromatic **2**:16, *17*, 36
  C major **2**:*36*
  pentatonic **2**:24–25, **3**:*24*, **5**:*21*, 22
  Phrygian and Dorian **8**:*5*
  and Pythagoras **1**:10
  whole-tone **2**:26, *32*
  See also modes
Scandinavia, nationalist composers
  2:29
Scarlatti, Alessandro **1**:43
Scarlatti, Domenico **1**:*43*–44, **2**:*66*
scat singing **5**:46, 55, **10**:63, 67
Schikaneder, Emanuel **1**:61
Schoenberg, Arnold **2**:35–36, **10**:19,
  44, 63–64
Schönberg, Claude-Michel **7**:47–48
schools
  early American singing **4**:8
  See also education, music
Schubert, Franz **2**:6–7, **10**:*18*
Schuller, Gunther **5**:66
Schumann, Clara **2**:8, 9, *14*
Schumann, Robert **2**:8–*9*, **10**:18
Schumann, William **4**:9
Scotland, mouth music **10**:63
"scratching" records **6**:58–59, **9**:*56*
Scriabin, Alexander **2**:27–28
Scruggs, Earl **4**:42, *43*
Seattle **6**:45
Second Great Awakening **4**:12
Sedaka, Neil **8**:30
Seeger, Pete **4**:24, *26*, 28, 31
Segovia, Andrés **1**:48, **9**:*15*–16
Segundo, Compay **3**:18
seis songs **3**:11
sel-sync **9**:*62*
semiprofessional musicians **8**:14–15
semitones **1**:11
sequencers **9**:52–53
serialism **2**:37, 38
  "total" **2**:57, 58
Sermisy, Claudin de **10**:*13*
session musicians **4**:48, **8**:22–23, 24
Sex Pistols **6**:*38*, 39–40, **8**:*35*
shaabi **3**:56
Shade, Will "Son" **5**:30
Shakur, Tupac **6**:*62*, 63
Shane, Bob **4**:25
Shangri-Las **6**:18
Shankar, Anoushka **3**:44
Shankar, Ravi **2**:61, **3**:42, *43*–44, 45
Shapis, Los **3**:26
Sharp, Cecil **4**:23
Shaver, Billy Joe **4**:57
Shaw, Artie **5**:54
shawm **1**:19, **9**:21, 34
sheet music **7**:18–19, 20, **8**:29, **10**:*48*
shekere **3**:*5, 7*
shells **1**:5
sheng **1**:*6, 8*, **3**:52
Shepp, Archie **5**:63, 65
Shirelles **6**:17, *18*
shofar **1**:12–13
shopping, and music **7**:*64*–65
Short, Bobby **7**:27
Shostakovich, Dmitri **2**:*51*–52, **7**:53
shouts **5**:11, 14
Show Boat (Kern) **7**:31
"show queens" **4**:58–59
Sibelius, Jean **2**:*48*–49
sight singing **1**:16
siku **3**:23
Silbermann, G.G. **9**:*37*–38
Silver, Horace **5**:*62*, 63
Simon and Garfunkel **3**:25, **4**:32, *33*

Simon, Paul **3**:67, **4**:32, *33*
Sinatra, Frank **5**:*54*, 55, **7**:66, **10**:9,
  46, 53–54
singer-songwriters **10**:54–55
Singh, Talvin **3**:*47*
singing **10**:4–9
  careers in **8**:19–20, *26*
  choral **10**:38–45
  jazz **5**:54–56
  world music **10**:*56–63*
  See also operas; songs
"singing cowboys" **4**:*44*
singles, record **8**:36, 37
singspiel **1**:36, 61, **7**:5–6
Siouxsie and the Banshees **6**:41
Sister Sledge **6**:55
sistrum **1**:5
sitar **3**:42, *43*–44
"Six, The" **2**:44–*45*, 46
ska **3**:37
slaves
  in America **3**:58, **4**:5, *20–21*, **5**:4–7,
    10–11, *12*, 20–21, 40, 41
  in Brazil **3**:26
  in the Caribbean **3**:32–33, 36, 39,
    58
  and salsa **3**:5, 7, 10, 11
Sledge, Percy **6**:48
Sleeping Beauty, The (Tchaikovsky) **2**:*17*
Slick, Grace **6**:29
Slits **6**:41
Sly and the Family Stone **6**:53, 54
Smashing Pumpkins **6**:45, 67
Smetana, Bedřich **2**:*22, 23*, 24
Smith, Bessie **5**:9, 14, 24–25, 29, 30,
  46, **10**:*49*
Smith, Clarence "Pine Top" **5**:48–49
Smith, Kate **10**:50
Smith, Mamie **5**:*25*–26, 29
Smith, Patti **6**:39
Smiths **6**:*44*
Smith, Will **6**:63, **8**:51
Smith, Willie "The Lion" **5**:48
Smokey Robinson and the Miracles
  6:20
Snoop Doggy Dogg **6**:*62*, 63
Snow, Hank **4**:40, 47
soca **3**:39, 41
Socarras, Alberto **3**:13
Socrates **8**:4
Solti, Sir Georg **8**:18
son **3**:8, 17
sonata form **1**:53, **8**:13
sonatas **1**:41, 53, **2**:64
Son de Solar **3**:15
Sondheim, Stephen **7**:11, 41, *42*
"songo" **3**:*16*
songs
  American Civil War **4**:14–16
  American folk **4**:18–35
  American Revolutionary War **4**:9–10
  lieder **2**:7, 14, **10**:18
  Native American **4**:5
  "popular" **10**:46–55
  protest **4**:28
  Romantic era **2**:5
  slave spirituals **4**:20–21
  solo **10**:10–19
  See also singing
songwriting factories **8**:29–30
sonnets **1**:26
Son Volt **4**:60, 61
Sony Corporation **8**:51
sopranos **10**:5–7, 37, 42
Sosa, Mercedes **3**:*31*
soukous **3**:62, 63, 64, 65
soul **5**:16–17, 19, **6**:46–52, 57
  and calypso *See soca*
sound cards **8**:64
sound effects **8**:62–64
Soundgarden **6**:45
Sound of Music, The (Rodgers and
  Hammerstein) **7**:40, *41*
sounds, of nature **1**:4
soundtracks, movie **7**:*62*, 63

source music **7**:52
Sousa, John P. **7**:9, **8**:*11*, **9**:24, 31
sousaphone **9**:*31*
South Africa **3**:65–67, **10**:*58*, 61–63
Soviet Union
  nationalist composers **2**:49–52
  See also Russia
Sovine, Red **4**:56
Spain, nationalist composers **2**:29, 48
Spears, Britney **6**:66
Spector, Phil **5**:18, **6**:*19*
speech rhythms **2**:43
Spence, Joseph **3**:38–39
Spice Girls **3**:19, **6**:66
spirituals **3**:39, **4**:12–13, 20–21,
  5:10–13
Sprechgesang **10**:63–64
Springsteen, Bruce **6**:*41*
square dances **4**:20, 39
Stamitz, Johann **1**:*58*
Stanley Brothers **4**:43–44
Starlight Express (Lloyd Webber)
  7:46–47
Starr, Ringo **6**:*22*, 27, **8**:*33*, **9**:*32*
Stax label **6**:48–49
steel bands **3**:40
Steiner, Max **7**:*53*, 55
Steppenwolf **6**:34–35
stereo sound **8**:59–60, **9**:57, 62
Stewart, John **4**:26
Stills, Stephen **4**:33
Stockhausen, Karlheinz **2**:58–*59*, **9**:46,
  10:64, 65
Stokowski, Leopold **1**:47, **2**:55
Stoller, Mike **8**:*30*
Stoneman, Ernest V. "Pop" **4**:37
Stooges **6**:39
Stookey, Noel "Paul" **4**:26
stop time **5**:43
Stradivari, Antonio **1**:41
Strait, George **4**:60
Strauss, J., "the elder" **2**:15, **7**:8
Strauss, J., "the younger" **2**:15, **4**:17,
  7:*7*, 8
Strauss, Richard **2**:20–21, **9**:45–46,
  10:*6*, 19, 32
Stravinsky, Igor **2**:*30*, 37, 39–41, 44,
  64
Strayhorn, Billy **5**:55
Streisand, Barbra **7**:27, **10**:55
stride piano **5**:47–48
stringed instruments **9**:6–18
Stuart, Marty **4**:60
Stubblefield, Clyde **8**:*32*
subidor **3**:10
Sub-Pop label **8**:*50*
Sudan **3**:56–57
Sugarhill Gang **6**:59
Summer, Donna **6**:56–57
Sun label **5**:32–33, **6**:10, 11, 12
Sun Ra's Arkestra **5**:65
Suppé, Franz von **7**:7
Supremes **6**:20–*21*
surf bands **6**:23–25
surnai oboe **3**:49
Sutherland, Joan **10**:7
Suzuki, Shinichi **8**:*4*, 8
swamp pop **4**:67
Sweden, nationalist composers **2**:29
swing **5**:15, 46, 50–54, 61, **10**:50
  Western **4**:47–48
  See also big bands
Sykes, Roosevelt **5**:32
symphonic/tone poems **2**:9, 20
symphonies **1**:*52*, 53, **2**:12–13
syncopation **1**:57, **4**:6, **5**:41
synthesizers **7**:57, **9**:43–45, *47*–51, 53

T

tabla **3**:44, 54, 56, 63
tablature **1**:*27*
Tad **6**:45

Tailleferre, Germaine **2**:44, *45*
Taj Mahal **3**:39, 59
Tallis, Thomas **1**:*25*
tambora **3**:33
tambur **3**:49
tambura **3**:43
Tampa Red **5**:31
Tangerine Dream **9**:50
tango **3**:*30–31*, **5**:67
Tanzania **3**:63
tape, magnetic **2**:56
tape loops **2**:60
tape operators **8**:*53–54*
tape recorders **8**:60–61, **9**:*60–66*
targeting **8**:39–40
tarka **3**:24
Tartini, Giuseppe **1**:43
Tatum, Art **5**:*48*, 58
Taylor, Cecil **5**:64
Taylor, James **4**:35
Tchaikovsky, Peter **2**:16–19, 64, **4**:16
teaching music **8**:24–27
techno **6**:65, **9**:51
teenagers, in the 1950s **6**:*8*
teen pop **6**:66
telegraphones **9**:*60*
television **4**:45, *49*, **7**:62
telharmonium **9**:43
tempo **1**:32
Temptations **6**:20, *46*, 51
tenors **1**:15, **10**:8, 28–31, *28*, 37, 42
Terry, Sonny **5**:32, 37
Têtes Brulées, Les **3**:*61*
Texas, blues **5**:28–29
Texas Playboys **4**:*47*
Texas Tornados **4**:53
Tex-Mex music **3**:21, **4**:*53*
Tharpe, Sister Rosetta **5**:*15*
Theile, Johann **1**:36
theme tunes **7**:*62*
theremin **2**:56, **7**:*57*, **9**:43–45
Third Stream **5**:66
Thomas, Ramblin' **5**:*31*
Thornton, Big Mama **5**:33
thrash metal **6**:37
throat-singing **3**:*53*, **10**:57–58
thumri **3**:46
tibia **1**:12
Tigres del Norte, Los **3**:22
Timbaland **6**:67
timbales **3**:13
timbrel **1**:12
timecodes **7**:58
time signatures **1**:16
timpani **9**:*31*, 33
Tin Pan Alley **5**:9, **6**:16–17, **7**:*18*, 19–20, **8**:29, 47, **10**:48
Tiomkin, Dimitri **7**:55
toasting **3**:38
Tobago **3**:33, 39, 40
tof **1**:12
Tommy (Townshend) **7**:*44*–45
tonada **3**:30
tonal music **2**:36
tone row **2**:*37*
tones, in Arab music **3**:54–55
Tong, Pete, DJ **8**:*57*
Toscanini, Arturo **2**:55, **8**:*18*
Tosh, Peter **3**:38
Touré, Ali Farka **3**:59
touring **8**:41–42, 43
Tower Records chain **8**:*40*
Townshend, Pete **7**:44
township jive **3**:66
trance **6**:65
transistors **9**:43
transposing instruments **9**:19, *26*
trautonium **9**:45–46

Travers, Mary **4**:27
Travis, Merle **4**:48
Travis, Randy **4**:47, 60
Travolta, John **4**:*58*, **7**:*44*
trebles **10**:5
tres **3**:6, 8, 9
triad chords **1**:*22*
Tribe Called Quest, A **6**:61
trills **1**:*33*
Trinidad **3**:*32*, 33, 39, 40
Tristan and Isolde (Wagner) **10**:*30*
trombone **2**:5, **9**:*28*
Tropicalismo **3**:29–30
Tropicana **3**:35
troubadours **1**:18–19, **10**:12
trouvères **1**:18
trumpet **1**:*6*, 11, **4**:6, **9**:*25–28*
Tryin' Times **3**:*53*
tuba **9**:30–31
Tubb, Ernest **4**:40, 41
Tucker, Sophie **7**:15
Tucker, Tanya **4**:59
Tudor, David **2**:*57*
Turkey **3**:57
Turner, Big Joe **5**:32, **6**:6
Turner, Ike **6**:5
Turner, Tina **6**:5
Turner, Nat **5**:*11*
Turpin, Tom **5**:41
Twain, Shania **4**:59, **6**:65
12-bar blues **5**:21, 42, **8**:13
12-tone composition *See* serialism
two-step dances **4**:63

U

U2 **6**:42–43
Ulloa, Francisco **3**:*34*
Uncle Tupelo **4**:61
United States
  cabaret **7**:26–27
  education in **8**:9–13
  nationalist composers **2**:52–53
  operetta **7**:9–11
  salsa **3**:13–17
  See also America
Unit Structures **5**:64
universities and colleges **8**:13
  teaching at **8**:25–26
Urfe, José **3**:9–10
urtexts **2**:66
Uruguay **3**:31

V

Valdez, Daniel **3**:22
Valens, Ritchie **3**:*23*, **6**:14, *15*
Van Gelder, Rudy **8**:49
Vangelis **7**:57
Van Halen **6**:36
Vanilla Ice **6**:63
Van Van, Los **3**:*16*, 17
Varése, Edgard **9**:45
variety shows *See* vaudeville
vaudeville **5**:*7*, 9, **7**:*12–18*, **10**:19, *47*–49
Vaughan, Stevie Ray **5**:39
Vaughan Williams, Ralph **2**:*46–47*, **10**:45
Velosa, Caetano **3**:29
Velvet Underground **6**:37–39
Venezuela, and salsa **3**:18–19
Ventura, Johnny **3**:34
veracruzano **3**:23
Verdi, Giuseppe **2**:18, **8**:*20*, **10**:*29*, *36*

verismo **2**:5, 18
verso **3**:30
vibraphone **5**:60, **9**:35
vibrato **2**:66
Vicious, Sid **6**:38
Victor label **5**:30, **8**:*46*
Vidal, Carlos **5**:57
videos, music **6**:64–65, **8**:*38*
vielle **1**:19
Vienna **1**:*52*, **2**:15, **7**:*7–8*
Vienna Boys' Choir **1**:54
Vietnam War **6**:25, *26*, 30
vihuela **9**:*14–15*
vina **3**:45–46
Vincent, Gene **6**:14
Vincentino, Nicola **10**:14
vingt-quatre violons du Roi **9**:8
viol **1**:31, 40–41
viola **9**:6, 9
violin **1**:40, 41, **9**:*6–9*
  single-stringed **4**:6
  teaching to play **8**:*4*, *8*
violin family **1**:40–41, **9**:6–11
violone **9**:11
virginal **4**:6, 7
Virgin label **8**:50
virtuoso performers **2**:9–10, **8**:15
Vitry, Philippe de **1**:16
Vivaldi, Antonio **1**:*41–43*, **9**:22
Vocalion label **5**:30
vocal jive **10**:62
vocoder **10**:65, 66
von Tilzer, Harry **7**:19
voodoo **3**:*34*

W

Wagner, Richard **2**:*14*, 15–16, 36, **10**:*30–31*, 33, *34*–35
Wagoner, Porter **4**:54
Wailer, Bunny **3**:38
Wailers **3**:37–38
Wakely, Jimmy **4**:44
Walker, "T-Bone" **5**:28–29, 32, 37
"walking bass lines" **5**:27
Walkman, Sony **9**:65, 66
Waller, "Fats" **5**:*47*, 48, **7**:44
Walt Disney, musicals **7**:36, 40–41, *49*
waltzes **2**:15, **4**:*63*, **7**:*7*, 8
Ward, Clara **5**:17
Warner-EMI label **8**:*50*
Warwick, Dionne **5**:*19*
Washington, Dinah **5**:34
Washington, Fredi **7**:25
Waters, Ethel **5**:56, **7**:26–27
Waters, Muddy **5**:27, 32, *34*, 35, 36–37, **6**:8
Watts, Isaac **5**:*11*, 12
Weather Report **5**:66
Weavers **4**:24
Weber, Carl Maria van **2**:*5–6*
Webern, Anton **2**:*37–38*
Webster, Ben **5**:52
Weill, Cynthia **8**:30
Weill, Kurt **7**:25, 35
Wells, Junior **5**:*31*, 35
Wells, Kitty **4**:50–*51*
Wells, Mary **6**:20
"We Shall Overcome" **4**:28, *29*, **5**:16
West, Dottie **4**:54
West Side Story (Bernstein) **7**:40, *41*
Wexler, Jerry **6**:48
Wheatstraw, Peetie **5**:32
White, George L. **5**:12, 13
Whiteman, Paul **5**:45
Whitfield, Norman **6**:51
Whitfield, Weslia **7**:27

Wilco **4**:60, 61
Wildman, Frank **7**:49
Wilhelmj, August **1**:48
Willaert, Adrian **1**:26, 30
Williams, Andy **10**:52–53
Williams, Bert **7**:16
Williams, Hank **4**:40, *45–46*
Williams, John (composer) **7**:*54*, 59
Williams, Lucinda **4**:60, 61
Williams, Marion **5**:17
Williamson, Sonny Boy (John Lee Williamson) **5**:34, 35
Williamson, Sonny Boy (Rice Miller) **5**:*34–35*
Williams, Robbie **8**:*32*
Willis, Kelly **4**:61
Wills, Bob **4**:*47*, 48
Wilson, Jackie **6**:19
Wilson, Teddy **5**:53, 58
wind instruments **9**:18–31
Winter, Johnny **5**:36, 39
Wizard of Oz, The **7**:*38*
Wolff, Francis **8**:49
Wolf, Hugo **10**:18, *19*
Wonder, Stevie **6**:53, **10**:66
Woodbridge, William Channing **8**:*9–10*
woodwind **2**:67, **9**:18–24
Work, Henry Clay **7**:19
work songs **5**:5, 7, 21–22
world music **3**:4–67, 42, **10**:*56–63*
Wright, Johnnie **4**:50
Wurlitzer **9**:46–47
Wynette, Tammy **4**:*46*, 47, 50, 52–53

X

xoomei **3**:53
X-Ray Spex **6**:41
xylophone **9**:*34*, 35

Y

yambu rhythm **3**:8
Yancey, Jimmy **5**:49
Yardbirds **6**:*31*
Yarrow, Peter **4**:26
Yearwood, Trisha **4**:59
Yes **6**:33
yina **3**:43
Yoakam, Dwight **4**:60
yodeling **4**:40, **10**:*58–59*
Yo mode **3**:*53*
Yonge, Nicholas **1**:26
Young, Lester **5**:52, **9**:924
Your Hit Parade **5**:53

Z

zamba **3**:31
zampoña **3**:24, 30
Zappa, Frank **6**:*30*
Zarlino, Gioseffo **1**:*22*
zarzuela **7**:5
Zawinul, Joseph **5**:66
Zeller, Carl **7**:7
Zelter, Carl F. **2**:63
Ziegfeld, Florenz **7**:*16*, 30–31
zither **1**:8, **9**:*16*
zouk **3**:35–36
Zouk Machine **3**:36
Zulus **10**:61–63
zydeco music **4**:66